Conversations on Science, Culture, and Time

Studies in Literature and Science
published in association with the
Society for Literature and Science

Titles in the series

Transgressive Readings: The Texts of Franz Kafka and Max Planck
by Valerie D. Greenberg

A Blessed Rage for Order: Deconstruction, Evolution, and Chaos
by Alexander J. Argyros

Of Two Minds: Hypertext Pedagogy and Poetics by Michael Joyce

The Artificial Paradise: Science Fiction and American Reality
by Sharona Ben-Tov

Conversations on Science, Culture, and Time
by Michel Serres with Bruno Latour

The Natural Contract by Michel Serres

Genesis by Michel Serres

MICHEL SERRES *with* BRUNO LATOUR

Conversations on Science, Culture, and Time

Translated by
Roxanne Lapidus

Ann Arbor
THE UNIVERSITY OF MICHIGAN PRESS

A CIP catalogue record for this book is available from the British Library.

Library of Congress Cataloging-in-Publication Data

Serres, Michel.
    [Eclaircissements. English]
    Conversations on science, culture, and time / Michel Serres
with Bruno Latour ; translated by Roxanne Lapidus.
        p.   cm. — (Studies in literature and science)
    ISBN 0-472-09548-X (alk. paper). — ISBN 0-472-06548-3 (pbk.: alk.
paper)
    1. Serres, Michel—Interviews. 2. Authors, French—20th century—
Interviews. I. Title. II. Series.
PQ2679.E679Z46513   1995
194—dc20   95-2706
                                                                  CIP

The publisher is grateful for partial subvention for translation from the
French Ministry of Culture.

Contents

Translator's Introduction

With the publication of *Hermès I. La communication* in 1969 Michel Serres set the tone for a controversial body of work that has evolved over the past twenty-five years through more than twenty books, which he sees as a series, a natural progression of his lifetime project of understanding what makes our world tick. In that first volume he introduced his main character and alter ego, the Greek god Hermes—the messenger—who, under Serres's pen, travels across time and space, making unexpected connections between seemingly disparate objects and events. These sometimes bewildering juxtapositions, which reflect Serres's unorthodox view of time itself, have baffled many critics and general readers.

It was with an eye to clarifying some of these sources of difficulty that sociologist Bruno Latour persuaded Michel Serres in 1991 to engage in the interviews that make up this book. Published in France under the title *Eclaircissements* (clarifications/illuminations), it was a best-seller and did much to dispel some of the misunderstandings surrounding Serres's work.

For English-speaking readers this translation should serve as an introduction to Serres, a provocative and unorthodox thinker whose major works are now available in English. His two most recent books are *The Legend of the Angels* (*La Légende des anges,* 1993) and *Atlas* (1994). An unabashed maverick, Michel Serres was elected in 1990 to the Académie Française.

Roxanne Lapidus
University of California, Santa Barbara

Background and Training

Bruno Latour: There is a Michel Serres mystery. You are very well known and yet very unknown. Your fellow philosophers scarcely read you.

Michel Serres: Do you think so?

BL Even though your books are technically on philosophy.

MS I hope so.

BL This is where I'd like some clarifications. Your books aren't obscure, but the way to approach them is hidden. You map out a path, you go everywhere—the sciences, mythology, literature—but at the same time you often cover up the traces that led you to your results. What I'm hoping for today is not that you will add more results, nor comment on your other books, but that you will help us to read them. In these conversations I hope that we may take up the thread that leads you to your results and that you will show me how you arrived there—that we may go behind the magician's curtain, that we may learn about your colleagues and see the underlying design of a body of work that doesn't appear to have one.

MS Scarcely eighteen months ago I would have refused this exercise; now I am willing to go along with it. I'll tell you why a little later.

BL My first difficulty is that you situate your works under the sign of Hermes. Now, Hermes is mediation, translation, multiplicity. But at the same time, especially in your later works, there is a side I would call Catharist—maybe that's not the right word—a will toward isolation, sepa-

ration, immediacy. So my first question has to do with your intellectual formation. You're not fond of debate; although famous, you are not well understood by your colleagues, and admittedly you often speak ill of them. What terrible thing happened to you, in your development, to make you so "gun-shy" of debate? What events pushed you into this solitary exercise of philosophy?

The War Generation

MS My contemporaries will recognize themselves in what I have to say first. Here is the vital environment of those who were born, like me, around 1930: at age six, the war of 1936 in Spain; at age nine, the blitzkrieg of 1939, defeat and debacle; at age twelve, the split between the Resistance and the collaborators, the tragedy of the concentration camps and deportations; at age fourteen, Liberation and the settling of scores it brought with it in France; at age fifteen, Hiroshima. In short, from age nine to seventeen, when the body and sensitivity are being formed, it was the reign of hunger and rationing, death and bombings, a thousand crimes. We continued immediately with the colonial wars, in Indochina and then in Algeria. Between birth and age twenty-five (the age of military service and of war again, since then it was North Africa, followed by the Suez expedition) around me, for me—for us, around us—there was nothing but battles. War, always war. Thus, I was six for my first dead bodies, twenty-six for the last ones. Have I answered you sufficiently about what has made my contemporaries "gun-shy"?

BL Yes, in part, indeed.

MS My generation lived through these early years very painfully. The preceding generation was twenty years old at the beginning of these events and, as adults, lived them in an active way, becoming involved in them. My generation could only follow them in the passivity of powerlessness—as child, adolescent—in any case, weak, and without any possibility of action. Violence, death, blood and tears, hunger, bombings, deportations, affected my age group and traumatized it, since these horrors took place during the time of our formation—physical and emotional. My youth goes from

Guernica (I cannot bear to look at Picasso's famous painting) to Nagasaki, by way of Auschwitz.

A written work, even an abstract one, cannot help remaining a distressed witness for a long time after such events, though it does not judge them. Perhaps what you are calling "Catharist" (did you know that my heritage descends directly from that tradition?) is the sound of lamentation that emanates from my books. This Jeremiah's cry comes from nowhere else but those shameful wars and the horrors of violence. The first woman that I saw naked was a young girl being lynched by a mob; this tragic influence forms not only the spirit and forgiveness but also the body and the senses.

Yes, when I read *Sein und Zeit* I feel the years before the war emanating from it—not through understanding or memory but physically—I irresistibly breathe the smell of it. Ask people my age who lived in France at that precise time; ask those who must have sung anthems in school to Marshal Pétain, before subsequently parading in celebrations of the Liberation, in honor of the Resistance—always flanked by the same adults. How could anyone in their position not feel scorn for those adults, not become old at age ten and experienced or wise? Ask them then if their nostrils don't immediately quiver with nausea in certain situations. I see (although I can't bear to look at them) the canvases of Max Ernst or of Picasso less as artistic works than as witnesses to that terrible era.

BL   That's the way that whole era thought of those events. That's no longer directly your formation.

MS That's easy for you to say, sitting comfortably here, but did that era really think about those events? The return to savagery—to the Minotaur, for Max Ernst, to Picasso's paganism—I still see these today as the atrocious forces unleashed on society during that era. Did they express that dangerous era, or did they create it? I was about to say, imprudently, that they produced it. Do I dare suggest that my generation still sees *Guernica* falling on painting and deconstructing it the way the Nazi planes bombarded the town?

BL   You're saying that these works are symptoms *of the evil and not an analysis of those symptoms?*

MS Yes, symptoms, and not reactions, either of defense or revolt. No, I have never recovered—I don't believe I'll ever recover from that horrible coming-of-age. Now that I am older, I am still hungry with the same famine, I still hear the same sirens; I would feel sick at the same violence, to my dying day. Near the midpoint of this century my generation was born into the worst tragedies of history, without being able to act.

Even today I can hardly bear evocations of that era, so much in fashion now among those who did not live through it. Even my own childhood photographs, happily scarce, are things I can't bear to look at. They are lucky, those who are nostalgic about their youth.

BL This explains why you are gun-shy—one of the "walking wounded" would be more accurate.

MS Note that, among those of my generation who suffered this coming-of-age, few have written about politics or assumed positions of power. Our active politicians come, more often, from the preceding or following generations.

This is due to those dark years; we suffocated in an unbreathable air heavy with misfortune, violence and crime, defeat and humiliation, guilt. Surely Western humanity, so advanced in its scientific and cultural accomplishments, had never gone so far in abomination.

This is not particular to one of the aggressors, to the exclusion of the other. The death camps were echoed by Nagasaki and Hiroshima, which were just as destructive of history and consciousness—in both cases in a radical way, by attacking the very roots of what makes us human—tearing apart not just historic time but the time frame of human evolution.

This tragic atmosphere began in 1936 (believe me, for I have a very good memory on this point—part of me has never left that era) with the war in Spain, with unspeakable horrors, and culminated with the bloody settling of accounts after the Liberation in 1945; the colonial wars and some episodes of torture brought this era to a close toward the early 1960s. In total, a good quarter-century. My generation was formed, physically, in this atrocious environment and ever since has kept its distance from politics. For us power still means only cadavers and torture.

The War Continues in Academia

BL But this historic moment is that of a whole generation. Let's talk more specifically about your own formation. You began your higher education in advanced math classes in 1947; you were accepted into the Naval Academy, from which you resigned in 1949; that same year you finished a degree in mathematics; you took preparatory classes and were accepted into the Ecole Normale Supérieure in 1952, and received your accreditation in philosophy in 1955. So that makes a good dozen years during which you were trained under the very best conditions.

MS Under the best and the worst. The contemporary postwar intellectual milieu, from 1947 to 1960, reacted in its own way—I don't know how to describe it now—to this series of events, and formed one of the most terroristic societies ever created by the French intelligentsia. I never tasted freedom in it. At the Ecole Normale Supérieure, like elsewhere, terror reigned. Powerful groups sometimes even held hearings there, and one was summoned before these juries and accused of this or that breach of opinion, termed an intellectual crime. A commando would go and summon pupils in their turn, to involve them in the judgment. The professors of philosophy were often Stalinists. I have memories of the Ecole that are almost as terrifying as those of the war of 1936 that brought Spanish refugees pouring into the southwest of France, of the war of 1939, of the camps, or of the Liberation in our rural areas.

BL I'm too young to have lived through that. I am of the generation following yours. But surely Marxism didn't reign supreme in Paris?

MS Almost. Once again I'd rather forget that milieu than have to describe it in detail. I'm not talking about intellectual content but about atmosphere. Terrorism reigned; I could even recount the sordidness of private life.

Thus, already scarred by historic events, I was later made gun-shy by the intellectual atmosphere.

BL I understand. So you had to escape from all that.

MS A piece of luck then intervened in my bad luck, which perhaps became my good luck, as happens in the vicissitudes of life and time. At the Ecole Normale, I lived in a world halfway between the

literary community and the scientific one. I suffered from loneli-
ness, but at the same time enjoyed a certain tranquillity. I first
studied the history of science and epistemology in order to have
peace; these disciplines sheltered me from political terrorism.

BL   Because you remained outside the contemporary debates?

MS No doubt. These parascientific disciplines did not excite me
but were like a monk's cell, since nothing was at risk.

BL   Since at least in them there were no disputes.

MS No, there were some, later, just as much as elsewhere, but no
one was interested at that time. Total isolation. Can you image
someone coming out of the very best institutional molds completely self-taught?

*BL   While we're on the subject of science, I wish you'd clarify this point.
You play up this scientific background a lot—can you describe exactly what
it was? You first studied at the Naval Academy from 1947 to 1949.*

MS Yes.

*BL   But later you abandoned the sciences, as you had abandoned the
Naval Academy a few years earlier.*

MS Not completely. I abandoned the sciences in order to study
philosophy because really, the shortest route—mathematics—led
to it, and I also chose it because of specific feelings about war and
violence, out of a sort of conscientious objection. Since then, certain things, and of course my ideas, have evolved from this point.

*BL   But you did enter the Naval Academy. You haven't told us why. It
wasn't out of militarism?*

MS No, but for more intimate and vital reasons. My father was a
fisherman and gravel dealer, a bargeman on the Garonne River,
and the son of a bargeman becomes a sailor—just as a river, at its
mouth, leaps into wider expanses—what could be more natural? I
had always known the calling of the water—I had been born on
the water; my family lived off the water. Family history has it that in
the great flood of 1930, when my mother was pregnant with me,
she was evacuated from our house by boat from the second-story
window. Thus, I had been afloat while still in the womb, and not
just in amniotic fluid! What's more, when you go to the Naval

Academy, you receive a scholarship. So—family heritage and economic necessity.

BL And then?

MS I resigned from the navy because I didn't want to serve cannons and torpedoes. Violence was already the major problem—has remained so, all my life. I pursued a degree in mathematics. In those years I had the good fortune to hear some very great professors of algebra and analysis—the kind who enable you to understand everything, tensors or structures, with a single gesture. Their style has remained with me as an ideal, in which rigorous truth is accompanied by beauty—rapid, elegant, even dazzling demonstrations, scorn for slow mediocrity, anger at recopying and recitation, esteem only for invention. Then from there I made a leap into literary studies, at the Ecole Normale, which I entered in 1952, and where that scientific formation and my interests assured me a kind of escape from the milieu—the sciences were not yet intellectually fashionable. I was always alone, with no one to talk to. I got used to it.

The disciples of Brunschvicg had disappeared; Cavaillès had died a hero in the Resistance. I had gone to England to read Russell and Wittgenstein. At that time—1953, if I remember rightly—I was thus one of the first to study mathematical logic and, a bit later, the first professor to teach it at the university, where there was no program of contemporary logic being taught under the aegis of philosophy. I was still both happy and unhappy—tranquil, certainly, but alone. No one was interested in that area, except a few rare mathematicians.

BL So you could have become the importer of mathematical logic and the philosophy of language. It's interesting to imagine what you might have become. Other possible Serres, as Leibniz would say.

MS It is, in fact, imaginable. In the 1950s and 1960s the intellectual atmosphere seemed to determine individuals. Marxism, which dominated, pushed people into careers on that royal road—the Marxist superhighway. The second superhighway, equally well established since before the war by Sartre and his disciples—not counting the influence of Merleau-Ponty at the time—was phenomenology, to put it briefly. This road already led to more precise works on Husserl (who was being translated in an appropriate style) or on Heidegger, who was entering into his worldly glory. The superhighways blazed out at the Ecole Normale Supérieure during the 1950s already pointed to who and what was going to appear.

BL I can understand easily why you learned nothing from Marxism, but phenomenology—you learned nothing from it?

MS Little, in sum. The mathematical beginnings of Husserl, his *Logical Investigations,* for example, interested me greatly, but I was turned off quickly by the disparity between the technical difficulty and the paucity of the results.

BL That was already your reaction at the time?

MS Yes. And in rereading him, it hasn't changed. One was therefore either a Marxist or a phenomenologist.

BL There was no third superhighway?

MS In fact, there were four routes. Along the length of the third one the social or human sciences were born or developed: sociology, psychoanalysis, ethnology, etc.

BL And the fourth superhighway, according to you?

MS The fourth was epistemology; no one followed it at the time.

BL But there was nonetheless a long tradition of French epistemology.

MS Epistemology in the French language—I mean the heritage of Duhem, Poincaré, Meyerson, and Cavaillès—was at that time more or less abandoned. I might have followed the latter, even though his work contained two kinds of obscurity—one stemming from a mathematics he had not quite mastered, the other from the phenomenology clothing it. On the other hand, Lautman, less fashionable since he hadn't worshiped at the shrine of Husserl, seemed a good epistemologist who understood or had a better grasp of the various stakes related to mathematical questions.

But this tradition was abandoned even more when English-language epistemology began to be imported—from Wittgenstein to Quine and beyond. That's the fourth superhighway. You can see them all, marked out.

A Self-Taught Man?

BL I wish you would be more precise. I'd like a glimpse of the professors who interested you, the influences you underwent. You need to tell us this so we can understand whom you are addressing when you write.

MS What contemporary author have I followed? None, alas. From the scientific point of view, Marxism put itself out of the running by sensational incidents, like the Lyssenko affair, in which a science student in our class committed suicide when he learned of the farce of the "new agriculture." At that time epistemology was taught by people who knew little about science, or only about very old forms of it. Having just left the sciences, why should I put myself in a milieu where they were talked about but not understood? Epistemology seemed to me to develop empty commentaries. Phenomenology didn't interest me either, for reasons of taste and economy.

BL For reasons of yield . . .

MS Why such high technology, for so little? Finally, the social sciences seemed to me to produce information, rather than knowledge. I was completely disoriented. This is why, in the end, I never found a mentor.

BL I understand. So, it's not just a manner of speaking?

MS Not at all. Alas—I had no professor, no school to join, no lobbying support group. I will say it again: although I went through the best schools, I became, in the end, a self-taught man. One of the secret strengths of the Ecole Normale, it must be admitted, is its ability to form independent beings, since it will take in wayfarers who turn away from the great superhighways. It was obvious that those who chose one of these would go far, but you must take into account a primitive need for freedom, for autonomy.

BL In spite of everything, you could have learned from one or the other of these schools of thought.

MS When I took my degree in mathematics, I too found myself in some sense on a superhighway, and my change of course and path, from the sciences to literature, was not made in order to choose a different superhighway.

The Three Scientific Revolutions

BL Before you explain to me this important change of course, I'd like to fully understand what you learned from the sciences. For you do not seem to have retained from them what epistemologists like Bachelard or Canguilhem, for example, have retained.

MS At that time a sublime surprise occurred in my studies: I wrote my thesis, under the direction of Bachelard, on the difference between the Bourbaki algebraic method and that of the classical mathematicians who had gone before. In the years 1953–54 I had studied the notion of structure, as used by algebraists and topologists. The question of how modern mathematics thus ignores its classical roots seemed to me at the time an interesting one to elucidate. In a certain sense it was already structuralism—well defined in mathematics—which I sought to redefine in philosophy, long before it came into fashion in the humanities a good decade later.

BL So, this was your first important scientific training?

MS Certainly. I have never recovered from this happy surprise, because through it I experienced a change in the universe, the profound transformation of a world—my first scientific and intellectual revolution. An extraordinary upheaval that changed my entire life! The algebra and analysis I had studied before entering the Ecole Normale were part of classical mathematics—continuous, in a certain way, with those of the seventeenth and especially the latter eighteenth centuries. I was then completely reeducated by certain scientists of my own age and academic class, who were structuralists in the algebraic sense—the right sense—of the term. They taught me what I know of modern mathematics—the notion of structure, modern algebra, topology—in short, what was going on in the Bourbaki seminar.

Imagine the experience: I was coming from history, from a half-dead past, as though dressed in lace and ruffles, and I entered a palace at the very moment when it was being rebuilt. I can only compare this thunderbolt—for so it truly felt to me—to the thrice-blessed moment when my teacher forced my left-handed self to write with the right hand: it was a dazzling discovery of a new world.

And this passage, this dual upbringing was decisive. Even if later I returned, with much more esteem, to the old mathematics.

BL   What really formed you then was the crisis in mathematics?

MS Crisis or renewal—or more a renaissance. During that same time the epistemological currents—either imported or internal to the French tradition—had no effect on what was actually taking place in the developing sciences, which was a considerable revolution in methodology. Invented by modern algebra and prewar topology, structuralism had not yet found its philosophical expression.

BL   Nor in the teaching of mathematics either, apparently?

MS Actually, yes. The teaching of mathematics was beginning to renew itself. But the epistemologists were working with already outdated sciences.

BL   Nevertheless, you wrote your thesis under Bachelard, and you were in some sense their hope at the time.

MS Yes, I wrote my thesis under Bachelard, but I thought privately that the "new scientific spirit" coming into fashion at that time lagged way behind the sciences. Behind mathematics, because, instead of speaking of algebra, topology, and the theory of sets, it referred to non-euclidean geometries, not all that new. Likewise, it lagged behind physics, since it never said a word about information theory nor, later, heard the sound of Hiroshima. It also lagged behind logic, and so on. The model it offered of the sciences could not, for me, pass as contemporary. This new spirit seemed to me quite old. And so, this milieu was not mine.

BL   It was the frontier of mathematical research that was decisive for you?

MS I will say it again: my true training consisted in witnessing—almost participating in—a profound change in this fundamental science. From there I became highly sensitized to analogous transformations in other domains—whence my swift acknowledgment of the importance of Brillouin's work, of information theory in physics, and, much later, of questions of turbulence, percolation, disorder, and chaos. As changes in attitude, these seemed to me as important as the revolution in algebraic method. Physics was changing, was revealing a whole new outside world. After fractal curves and strange attractors, you no longer feel the same wind, no longer see the same waves or the same shores as before.

A similar storm was blowing, shortly afterward, in the life sciences. Those who would become biochemists understood rapidly that their own revolution would come, after information theory, from the questions posed in Schrödinger's *What Is Life?* and in France from Monod and Jacob's discoveries. Now, that was certainly not what epistemology was teaching about biology.

BL Right. It was cells and the reflex arc.

MS And other, perfectly respectable things too, which we should know or at least preserve in our memory, to prepare for the future, which will spring up from some unpredictable place. But things which, at the time, became abruptly outdated.

Once again the epistemologists didn't follow.

BL So, it is true that you had no mentors, but there were those who influenced you—your scientific colleagues, engaged in projects of renewal unnoticed by philosophy?

MS Yes. All things considered, I was formed by three revolutions. First, the mathematical transformation from infinitesimal calculus or geometry to algebraic and topological structures; that was my first school—the bifurcation of the two mathematics, from which we emerged with a whole new way of thinking. The second was in the world of physics. I had learned classical physics, and suddenly here was quantum mechanics, but especially information theory, from which we emerged with a completely new world.

BL You learned that at the Ecole Normale, in a hands-on way?

MS There and elsewhere, later. One of my friends had lent me, in 1959, Brillouin's *Science and Information Theory,* which had just been published. From it I understood that Brillouin was a veritable philosopher of physics—an authentic physics and a philosophy at the same time, somewhat like thermodynamics, from which, in fact, it sprang.

The third revolution came later, from having known Jacques Monod and from having had him as a friend for a long time—a wonderful friend, who taught me contemporary biochemistry. I was very close to him, since he asked me to read his manuscript of *Chance and Necessity*. That was my third school, from which I emerged with a changed life. But that was much later. To give you an idea of how much later—at the very end of the 1960s my professors of philosophy were still attacking Monod, and for unsound ideological reasons.

BL And none of these revolutions were registered by epistemology?

MS Not that I'm aware of.

BL Nor did epistemology register the violence of the era you were speaking of earlier?

MS No. Thus, my formation took place outside the system of ordinary programs and outside the social milieu that gives rise to what the press calls "mainstream intellectual movements." For better or for worse—who can say?—I have lived and worked outside of what formed most of my contemporaries.

Thus, I developed the habit, which you may find strange, of learning philosophy elsewhere than in the places where it was allegedly taught. I learned almost everything on the outside and almost nothing on the inside. Yes—we can safely put it that way— everything on the outside, almost nothing on the inside.

BL So, it is a problem of intellectual situation and a crisis in the sciences. I understand why you have so little faith in what social histories say about the sciences. If we were to read about the intellectual milieu of the period, we would not understand anything about what had influenced you?

MS Practically nothing, in fact. Unless you were to examine closely what was going on—in reality, I mean. In fact, what do we call the "intellectual milieu"? You speak of "situation"—I was straddling literature and the sciences. On one side nothing was going on except the mandatory superhighways and scholasticism; on the other there were unceasing revolutions in which I was, each time, present, witnessing, involved.

This dazzled me like a landscape of high contrasts or drove me into an unsettling disequilibrium. I had one foot on solid ground, philosophy, where nothing had changed since before the war, and the other foot on a conveyor belt that was advancing at changing speeds! How could you not run the risk of falling on your face? Thus, I reacted to the revolution in modern mathematics by my first thesis, already mentioned, on algebraic and topological structures, in 1953–54. Then I reacted to information theory, as can be seen abundantly in my books, and, finally, I reacted to biochemistry.

BL So, those were the turning points, for you?

MS After the war, yes—I am sure of it.

BL Because, if I continue to imagine other possible Serres, you might have said, "There's nothing more to be done in literature; let's just analyze these scientific revolutions." You would have left philosophy to its own violence and its predetermined lines of inquiry.

MS Yes, I could have, as you say, but what interested me, what still interests me more than anything else, was—is—philosophy.

In the 1960s I published a short article on epistemology, "The Quarrel of the Ancients and the Moderns," in which I conclude (and for the rest of my life) that this kind of commentary—often redundant and inferior to its object—will never interest me again. It appeared in my book *Hermès I. Communication*—in other words, very early. In it I take a critical inventory of a book by Edouard Le Roy on classical mathematics, and I return to the findings I had made in my thesis: either science must develop its own intrinsic epistemology, in which case it is a question of science and not of epistemology, or else it's a matter of external annotation—at best redundant and useless, at worst a commentary or even publicity.

Why? Because the revolutions and transformations to which I had been an enthusiastic witness came most often from an internal, truly philosophical meditation—from science considered in the light of its preceding state. In other words, authentic epistemology is the art of inventing, the springboard for passing from the old to the new.

From that point on I abandoned definitively any idea of commenting on the three revolutions. As you say, I could have taken up a career as an epistemologist, as a commentator on the structural revolution, on the information revolution, on the biological revolution—but what would be the difference between that and a journalistic account?

BL So, you could have written a new version of Bachelard's The New Scientific Spirit?

MS Yes. I almost set out on that route, at a certain moment, but shouldn't a philosopher's work differ from that of a journalistic chronicler, who announces and comments on the news?

BL Or you could have decided simply to become a scientist.

MS I had been in the sciences. I had abandoned them.

BL I mean you could have decided to abandon philosophy and to stick with mathematics—to continue.

MS Once again, I left the sciences and arrived at philosophy for very precise reasons. Thus, I wanted—needed—to stay there.

Hiroshima and the Passage from the Sciences to the Humanities

BL Excuse me, but we have scarcely talked about these reasons, so far. For all that you have said about the milieu of the humanities, it's not apparent why you chose to stay there. What made you "gun-shy" in both the sciences and in the humanities?

MS My decision to switch from the sciences to the humanities was both beneficial and a total loss. This decision came after my departure from the Naval Academy in 1949 but also following my deep interest in mathematics, which had led quickly to questions that were specifically philosophical.

BL So, something was happening in the sciences that forced you to abandon them after 1950?

MS Of course, an enormous event—a revolution of a whole other order than the other three—was taking place at that time between knowledge and morality. My resignation from the Naval Academy was only a private and minuscule consequence of this. Since the atomic bomb, it had become urgent to rethink scientific optimism.

I ask my readers to hear the explosion of this problem in every page of my books. Hiroshima remains the sole object of my philosophy. Let's return to the beginning of our conversation: the contemporary jeremiad that we were talking about earlier doesn't lament over small personal misfortunes but, rather, over a universal situation, brought about by a historic drama. In it what does the individual matter? Yes, one after the other all the sciences were changing, but, more profoundly, their relations with the world and with mankind were changing.

BL Can you explain this external transformation that was taking place alongside the internal ones we talked about earlier?

MS Let's back up to make the link between intellectual formation and historical circumstances. I belong to the generation that questions scientism. At the time one could not work in physics without having been deafened by the universal noise of Hiroshima. Now, traditional epistemology still was not asking any questions on the relationship between science and violence. Everything was taking place as if the scientific Ivory Tower were inhabited by good children—naive, hard-working, and meticulous, of good conscience and devoid of any political or military horizons. But weren't they the contemporaries of the Manhattan Project, which prepared the bomb?

BL But, according to what you have said, scientists' enthusiasm was also at its highest point.

MS Absolutely yes, and also absolutely no. Because that time was the beginning of "Big Science," to use the jargon of the day, with all its efficiency, but, on the other hand, even before the war certain physicists had abandoned science out of wariness of collaborating with what later became the atomic bomb. No doubt you are familiar with the fascinating story of Ettore Majorana, the Sicilian atomic scientist whose disappearance was recounted by Sciascia. He preferred to abandon everything rather than continue working in that path. I'm tempted to say that, on his own scale, he resigned from physics in the same way that I resigned from the scientific and military schools.

BL Did he have a direct influence on you?

MS No, that never happens as described in books. Neither one knows the other, but the whole world acts together, as though guided by an invisible hand.

BL So, you abandoned epistemology for the same reason that you abandoned the sciences, and you left the sciences for the same reason that you resigned from the Naval Academy.

MS In a certain sense, yes. The first revolutions concerned methodology, but the last one involved morality, sociopolitics, philosophy. For the first time since its creation, perhaps since Galileo, science—which had always been on the side of good, on the side of technology and cures, continuously rescuing, stimulating work and health, reason and its enlightenments—begins to create real problems on the other side of the ethical universe.

A few years later, speaking of a completely different science, Jacques Monod said to me, and I remember his exact words, spoken to me the very day before his death:

> I used to laugh at physicists' problems of conscience, because I was a biologist at the Pasteur Institute. By creating and proposing cures, I always worked with a clear conscience, while the physicists made contributions to arms, to violence and war. Now I see clearly that the population explosion of the third world could not have happened without our intervention. So, I ask myself as many questions as physicists ask themselves about the atomic bomb. The population bomb will perhaps prove more dangerous.

Monod himself, for whom knowledge was the essence of ethics, before leaving us, asked himself the question of scientific responsibility.

Between 1940 and 1960, while the power of science was increasing, the importance of such questions was also growing, in parallel. But the books on the philosophy of science contained nothing about it.

BL This passage is fundamental, but in the beginning did it remain instinctive?

MS I made the passage from science to philosophy in my twenties, gropingly, and I find reasons that are more and more strong, lucid, and conscious as time goes by.

BL Had science professors had this crisis of conscience?

MS Absolutely. In the 1950s older colleagues whom I could name stopped their activities in nuclear physics and reoriented themselves, even in disciplines less current, for reasons of conscience.

So, I was formed intellectually by science's internal revolutions, and philosophically by the relationship—internal and external—between science and violence. The latter question has dominated everything up to this point—both my life and my studies.

BL But at the same time, when you turned toward the humanities and the social sciences . . .

MS I found nothing there that addressed these questions.

Simone Weil, Philosopher of Violence

BL No one at all?

MS Actually, yes. I had read Simone Weil, the first philosopher really to speak of violence in all its dimensions—anthropological, political, religious, and even scientific. None of my books ever really abandons this question, which came from my historic and intellectual experience, of course, but which was thought about for the first time with great intensity by this extraordinary woman, whose work I encountered at the time it appeared.

BL This is a thread that is becoming more and more important in your recent work but which is important in your formation—your religious education.

MS As to that, I was formed by Simone Weil.

BL What were the intermediaries that brought you to that point?

MS When I was studying mathematics, at one point—I don't know how—Weil's *Gravity and Grace* appeared on my table. It is largely because of this book that I resigned from the Naval Academy and that I left the sciences for philosophy. Simone Weil analyzes the relations between science and society in other books; indeed, she was the only philosopher who really influenced me, in the sense you give that word.

BL But your father was a convert to Catholicism.

MS Yes, but much earlier, under the hail of shells at Verdun. He was born into an atheist family, in the anticlerical tradition of the Southwest (he was named Valmy, after a battle in the French Revolutionary Wars!). The experience of the 1914–18 war, for which he enlisted at age seventeen, brought him to that religion, which in fact he practiced with the fervor of a convert.

BL But you?

MS My family owned no other book except the Gospel.

BL But from the point of view of your upbringing? Did you participate in the Action Catholique, *for example, which was the other great anti-Marxist force and which played such an important role for so many intellectuals?*

MS Try to discover from whence come those rare men who behave rightly during a dark and violent period. Have you ever asked yourself what protects someone from the dangers, deviations, or crimes of a given ideology, if not a religion and its inner anchor?

BL But you—were you in any of those movements?

MS Very little. Your questions seem to seek social, intellectual, and political influences, and you find here a solitary and disoriented provincial. I lived a thousand kilometers from Paris, in a countryside that, as I described in *Detachment,* knew nothing of history. Indeed, I knew and still know places and people who exist without history, or with very little of it—in the sense that Parisian intellectuals give this word. This is why I am astonished to hear questions about influences; the villagers and sharecroppers of my childhood in Quercy or the central Garonne had never participated in history, which they did not seek to understand, from pure disinterest, or which they only encountered through conscription and military service—implacably hated.

And I am not discounting the real though silent heritage of Catharism in this region. Indeed, if my father could have expressed it, he would have said—because he believed it and, thus, lived in that certitude—that the social world is in the hands of the powers of evil. A part of me still believes it and has lived it all my life—irresistibly, as uncontradicted evidence. The higher one goes on the ladder of social recognition, the closer one comes to the most evil forces.

Of course, friends around us received magazines and passed them on to us. It was perhaps through *Esprit* that I knew Simone Weil and the first philosophical reverberations of Hiroshima or the war.

But I am driven by a strong disinclination to "belong" to any group, because it has always seemed to require excluding and killing those who don't belong to the sect. I have an almost physical horror of the libidinous drive to belong. You will notice that this drive is rarely analyzed as such, since it supports all ambitions and serves up the most widespread morality.

Finally, it goes without saying that after a certain age, questions of upbringing lose more and more of their pertinence, as a person becomes the father of himself—as he takes responsibility for his decisive and definitive education. Only the lazy and the infirm remain dependent on their initial upbringing—an ailment that should be treated.

BL I have not had the same experience of violence, but I think I understand what you are saying.

MS Weighing those early years in the balance, I can say that I only learned to disobey. All the events that took place around me only left me with a taste for disobedience. I had the impression, during my student years and at the university, that the war was not over, that the Occupation was still going on, and that therefore one still had to resist, still had to go underground, still had to say *no* to the current conventional wisdom that influenced careers or guided what the press calls "the great intellectual movements." It's terrible or tragic, but perhaps also lucky, to go through the best institutions of learning and research and only learn there to rebel. Time wasted or well spent—who can say?

BL So, you had to manage on your own?

MS In the sense that at a certain age I decided to establish myself on my own, no matter what the price of this whim. I had no legitimation to set up shop, since legitimate thinking was channeled into the superhighways, but there was no other solution. I was going to seek my own way. I did not have a lot of means, perhaps, but through work I would go where I could, and at least I would remain free.

Have you noticed to what extent freedom of thought remains rare, even among philosophers who celebrate it in the texts they write about? This is the reason for the idiosyncrasy that seems to amaze you: the wounds received in the environments first of war and then of polemics caused the almost savage reaction of setting up one's tent in a distant place, even if the spot was desertlike— since there was no way to go elsewhere.

Do you sometimes go for walks in the country? You cannot approach the houses, because watchdogs, usually ferocious, keep you at bay. I have a panic-stricken fear of those beasts, which my contemporaries seem to prefer to their children. So, you find yourself forced to blaze a trail off the beaten paths, to avoid bites and barks. Anyone on the outside seeing you proceed has a hard time understanding where you are coming from, where you are headed, and which way you are going, since you continually change direction—but he will understand very well if he sees and hears the dogs.

When you have no affiliations and want above all to avoid them, when you have no home and cannot live anywhere, you are very much obliged to begin a project. All my life I have had the distressful feeling of wandering in the desert or on the high seas. And when you are lost and it is stormy, you quickly feel the need to build a raft or a boat or an ark—even an island—solid and consistent, and to supply it with tools, with objects, with shelters, and to people it with characters . . . doesn't philosophy consist of such a series of domestic improvements? Later, whoever wants can seek shelter there.

From Philosophy to the Humanities

BL But once you set up on your own, as you say, we encounter a new element we haven't talked about—literature. You don't just pass from the sciences to philosophy, but from philosophy to the humanities, skipping over epistemology and the history of philosophy.

MS Let's talk, in fact, about the role of the history of philosophy, which is so important in French studies. What's important, so it's said, is to know Plato, Kant, Hegel, Husserl, and others. Certainly, one should know them by studying them carefully—I agree. But the goal of teaching is to have teaching cease; the goal of repetition is to be delivered from it; the goal of copying is to be done with recopying.

So, there is nothing to equal the history of philosophy, especially as training—except not having to do it anymore when one has done it. I put a lot into studies on Leibniz, Descartes, Lucretius, Nietzsche, and Kant and a lot into huge publishing efforts, and now I believe I have earned the freedom to think on my own.

BL You are always ambiguous about this question of freedom of thought, since you have read everything but act as though you hadn't.

MS That's an excellent definition of good training—in philosophy and elsewhere! To start by being familiar with everything, then to start forgetting everything.

On the other hand, we must define a perversion of the idea of what's important, what's serious. Repetition is serious in the beginning, but later it is not. It doesn't remain so. It is only serious during apprenticeship. Unfortunately, you are not taken seriously when you try to reflect on the basis of it. I instinctively had the opposite idea. Philosophy's focus on its history can become prejudicial to the independent exercise of philosophy, although it is necessary and excellent as training. Interpretation is only the beginning of philosophy. In a certain sense, students should not stay in school. The only serious thing is invention.

BL But in spite of all this, you read a lot and can quote extensively.

MS The more one writes, the less one reads—it's a question of time. But I stress: an authentically philosophical book is often distinguishable from a learned book. The latter, loaded with quotes and footnotes, struts its erudition; it flourishes its credentials in the academic milieu, brandishes its armor and its lances before its adversaries. It is a social artifact. How many philosophies are dictated solely by the preoccupation with being invulnerable to criticism? They present themselves as fortresses, usually sheltering a lobbying support group. In the wide open spaces of fear, only trepidation reigns.

I have come to believe that a work achieves more excellence when it cites fewer proper names. It is naked, defenseless, not lacking knowledge but saturated with secondary naïveté; not intent on being right but ardently reaching toward new intuitions.

A university thesis aims at the imitable; a plain and simple work seeks the inimitable.

BL I like footnotes and so do not share your opinion, but I understand that you have never wanted to work in the history of philosophy.

MS At first yes, later no. In the end maybe yes. I wanted to place myself on a sort of watershed by rereading the entire philosophical tradition as it had been taught to us, in the light of this extraordinarily fresh thinking that was renewed by the revolutions I just spoke of. It was imperative to look again at a large part of the classics, in their entirety, in a new way. This is an important task that seems never to have been achieved.

BL But why didn't you scorn literature? For one can imagine another Serres who becomes a technician of philosophy, even of a renewed philosophy, and who nonetheless would not be interested in the cultural tradition, in literature . . .

MS I can't give a reasoned answer to this—only a personal one. I have always been excited by Greek and Latin culture. My references in philosophical matters are more often to Plato, to the pre-Socratics.

BL Since when? At the Ecole Normale? Always?

MS Almost. Since secondary school. Temperamentally, I have always been a Hellenist.

Another idiosyncrasy: I must be grounded in French language and taste. Hypertechnicality in philosophy makes me laugh or cry but not think; it's useless, redundant, harmful. This is not something recent. Right after the war, when people were talking about *noetico-noematic* structures, and about thetic or nonthetic consciousness, it seemed totally ridiculous to me. At the Ecole Normale certain presentations, bristling with a hypertechnical vocabulary, left me gasping with laughter. My early sense of being terrorized gave way to outbursts of mirth. Why this reaction? Because of my scientific training. In mathematics you know why you use a technical word—because it's a shortcut. It's much easier and quicker to say "ellipsis" than "a kind of elongated circle with two centers."

BL That is, in fact, an ellipsis.

MS Bravo, yes, linguistically it's true. But at that time nearly every time someone used a technical word in metaphysics it was in order to talk more, not to say less. Never out of economy, almost always for more output. So then, the voluptuousness of technicality occupies the entire discourse, constitutes it, and becomes extravagant and parasitic, while mathematics pursues the opposite goal—economy and speed.

Furthermore, in these two types of discourse an effect of terrorism is achieved, dividing those who use these words (I say "use," not "understand") and the uninitiated. Ultratechnical vocabulary breeds fear and exclusion.

BL But your style is considered difficult, exclusive.

MS Nonetheless, I remain as much as possible in everyday language—I simply use it in all its amplitude. And an author who uses lots of words is usually considered difficult. He forces readers to refer to the dictionary, but, in reviving language, he puts new life into it.

The patient and reasoned use of ordinary language in philosophy seems to me to guarantee accessibility and harmony. It provides the equivalent of a secular ideal. For technical language divides people into lobbying support groups—into sects that wage war on one another, treating one another as heretics. The particular style of teaching philosophy in France for the last hundred years comes from this secular ideal. Everywhere else, sects occupy entrenched camps.

Formed by the war, by all the wars, I love and seek peace, which seems to me the ultimate good.

BL And so literature appealed to you?

MS In some respects a well-told story seems to me to contain at least as much philosophy as a philosophy expressed with all this technical voluptuousness.

BL Where does this trait of yours come from? It's your trademark. This idiosyncrasy does not seem very French.

MS Come, now. If Plato did not turn up his nose at old wives' tales, myths and literature, neither do Montaigne, Pascal, Leibniz (who usually wrote in French), or Diderot hesitate to use these materials, which are both clear and obscure.

BL Yes, but such tales did not figure at all in the French philosophy you could have encountered, especially during that period.

MS Philosophy can be summed up in little stories. Was it the Gospel that taught me this, by its constant use of parables?

BL Paraboles, meaning both parables and parabolas, coming after the ellipsis—this is very appropriate!

MS Philosophy is profound enough to make us understand that literature is even more profound.

BL So, this trait, you got it in some sense from your love of Greek and from reading the Gospel?

MS From frequenting French-language authors as well. Furthermore, perhaps I loved Plato because of this continual mixture of pure mathematics and shepherds' folktales. But this mixture is common to the best philosophers. Pascal's *Pensées* and Leibniz's *Theodicy* are teeming with playlets and parables—and so, even, is Hegel.

BL In any case, you didn't get it from the intellectual milieu, which is steeped in jargon?

MS I don't like jargon. In fact, the more I write and the older I become, the more I abandon it, by a progressive effort toward the greatest possible clarity. Technical vocabulary seems even immoral: it prevents the majority from participating in the conversation, it eliminates rather than welcomes, and, further, *it lies* in order to express in a more complex way things that are often simple. It doesn't necessarily lie in its content but in its form, or, more precisely, in the rules of the game it imposes. You can almost always find a lucid way to express delicate or transcendent things. If not, try using a story!

Have you noticed, historically, that philosophy becomes intoxicated with technicality as soon as it enters academia, while its expression becomes simplified as soon as it leaves there? For this reason we are living today (and even more so in the United States than in Europe) closer to the Middle Ages than to the salons of the Age of Enlightenment.

BL Generally speaking, the humanities have always been present for you; you have always had them with you like a repertoire . . .

MS Because of their clarity, because of their beauty, yes. I have never ceased to seek beauty. Often beauty is the light of truth, almost its test. Style is the sign of innovation, of passage into new territory.

BL But how did you get the idea of applying the sciences from which you came to these literary texts? For, if I continue to imagine my different possible Serres, I see one who engages in technical philosophy but who pursues literature as a simple hobby. How did you get the idea to cross their forces?

MS That's another question. It's a matter of schizophrenia—a naughty, bad word—of not saying in private what one expounds in public.

BL What do you mean?

MS The political militants of the period never said in private what they were saying in public, because they knew perfectly well what was going on in Eastern Europe. Likewise, scientific theory was helpful in the workplace, but literature and the arts filled leisure and recreation time.

We were witnessing the beginnings of the breakup of culture, which did not allow for synthesis. For example, at the Ecole Normale we heard criticisms of interdisciplinarity, for ideological reasons. I never could appreciate this fragmentation nor, in general, the negative values so esteemed by my contemporaries. As a child of the war and its bombings, formed by the horror of the concentration camps, I have always preferred to construct, or put together, rather than destroy. I am glad that there are rapports between *things* and us (as the "subjects" of study); the god Hermes had already converted me to this. And don't take the word *construct* necessarily in the sense of hard stones—I prefer turbulent fluids or fluctuating networks.

Furthermore, the exercise of philosophy cannot be separated from a certain conception of totality. Yes, a philosopher should know everything, should have lived everything and understood everything—the sciences, hard and soft, their history, but also that which is *not* science, the entire encyclopedia, with no exclusions.

What underpins philosophy is not this or that partial science but the active totality of knowledge, as a totality. One only becomes a philosopher late in life—unlike scientists, who start inventing in their youth—because one must pass almost all of one's life in preparation. The time of apprenticeship is immense, because it must encompass everything. As for experience, one must have traveled in the world and in society; one must know the country-side and social classes, different latitudes and cultures. For knowl-edge, the encyclopedia, and for life, the world. From formal logic to the five senses and from Rome to parasitology—inevitably, the philosophical work reflects this totality. It excludes nothing; better yet, it attempts to include everything.

And at a certain point it all gels. I'm wishing and hoping for it still—as you see, I'm still in a fluid state! So, one must be inter-ested in everything. Try to name a single great philosopher who defies this description. So why would I exclude literature?

BL So, in response to my question about a hobby, you are saying that the humanities cannot be a pastime or a recreation?

MS That's right. One would have to hold them in low esteem to make them a simple hobby. Like behavior, culture is even more clumsy if one only works on it on Sunday.

BL But, technically, at a certain moment you still had to take a shortcut from mathematics to stories (to put it in a nutshell). Now, then, you could not have been impelled toward this by a milieu, since no such milieu existed. Even in your first writings on Hermes we find this characteristic feature. You must have discovered it. Now, of course, we can see that perhaps it was a matter of a French tradition, a philosophical tradition, but we have learned this from you. At the time how did you arrive at this?

MS A little while ago we were wondering what might protect a person from all criminal ideologies. Do you think that pure and simple scientific rationality is enough to make one lead a happy, responsible, and good life? What positive science, what logic, what formal abstraction can bring one to reflect on death, love, others, the circumstances of history, violence, pain or suffering—in sum, on the old problem of evil? If culture is only useful for life's Sundays, for lining up in museums and applauding concerts, I will gladly leave it to the various cultural snobberies. No—the ques-tions fomented since the dawn of time by what we call the humanities help rethink those asked today, about and because of the sciences.

This is behind our pressing need for a meeting point, for a link, for a synthesis, in the very place where now there is only schizophrenia, fragmented culture or destruction. At the Ecole Normale, which was nonetheless founded so that students of science and literature could meet for mutual enrichment and cross-fertilization, the separation was already in place. The scientific experts were uncultured, and the so-called cultured were ignorant. The decadent taste for fragmented culture simply reflects the scholastic division between students in math and in the liberal arts—the social distance between the efficient engineers and those who would soon be reduced to the role of vaudeville entertainers.

BL So, it's scientists' ignorance of the humanities and humanists' ignorance of the sciences that make any philosophical reflection impossible?

MS Since you stress training—and my training—I will say that I have tried to remain on the bridge between the two shores. Having passed two baccalaureate exams (elementary math and philosophy), three undergraduate degrees (mathematics, classics, and philosophy), and two admissions competitions for the *grandes écoles,* in science and in literature, I had become a half-caste or a quadroon, commingling the liberal arts student with the math student, pouring differential equations into Greek exercises and vice versa. Cross-breeding—that's my cultural ideal. Black and white, science and humanities, monotheism and polytheism—with no reciprocal hatred, for a peacemaking that I wish for and practice. It's always peace, for a child of war. Add to that the fact that as a corrected left-handed person, I write with my right hand but work with the left. I now call this a completed body. Never any fragmentation or schizophrenia. Don't imagine that I advocate this kind of upbringing because it was my own. On the contrary, all my life I have attempted to follow its rule.

Lots of authors practice the same connectedness. Plato was not afraid to mix problems of geometry with quotes from Pindar; Aristotle addresses medicine and rhetoric; Lucretius writes hymns to physics; as analysts, Leibniz and Pascal write with perfection; Zola novelizes genealogy; Balzac, La Fontaine, Jules Verne—what author doesn't do it?

The separation between the scientific ideal and literary temptation (I use theological and moral vocabulary intentionally) is of fairly recent date, at least since the Enlightenment, and perhaps only since the era of the contemporary university. In *Les Atomes* Perrin still quotes from Lucretius.

Finally, philosophers with a good knowledge of the hard sciences and of the classics—armed with rigor and culture—will never be taken in by folly or ideologies. I often deplore the fact that this kind of training has disappeared, giving way to the exclusive reign of the social sciences.

Bachelard and Auguste Comte

BL We know now that all these authors were in fact making this link, but we know this retrospectively, in part thanks to you. The dominant epistemology of the period did the opposite: it separated letters and science. To finish up on your background and training, I would like to understand your conflictual relationship with the epistemologists. You were at first considered by them as one of their own.

MS Yes, I knew a bit about the sciences.

BL Thus this career, this possible Serres, was interrupted brutally, in a certain sense.

MS Yes, quite suddenly. I cheerfully sawed off the branch on which I might have sat. As a useless path, epistemology requires one to learn science in order to commentate it badly, or worse, in order to recopy it. Scientists themselves are better able to reflect on their material than the best epistemologists in the world—or at least more inventively.

BL I'm trying to explore all the possible Serres, the Serres that we have missed out on. As an epistemologist, you could have set an example of mathematical logic.

MS I did so in the beginning, quite a bit. After being the first to teach it in a department of philosophy, as I told you, I abandoned it, because it seemed to be a lesser mathematics. Its landscape is less sumptuous. To dedicate one's life to "*p* implies *q*"—what a bore! And what a restriction on thought!

There remained the history of science. I made it my trade, to earn my daily bread, and as an entrée into an institution, nothing more. A trade is already a good and joyful thing, you know. In this discipline one encounters magnificent problems—for example, the origins of geometry. How did the abstract come to a group of men at a given, well-known moment? We must never stop reflecting on this question, which reverberates in nearly all my books. If we really knew how to resolve it, we would make real progress in philosophy.

BL   Wait a minute. You nonetheless had colleagues in this domain of the history of science—there was a French tradition of the history of science . . .

MS Two, in fact. On the one hand, the classical tradition, in the footsteps of Pierre Duhem and Jules Tannery, who was the first, in fact, to work on the Greek origins of geometry. On the other hand, Bachelard and his followers, who occupied a dominant position over the other tradition. I described earlier Bachelard's delay in defining a new scientific spirit—a delay made for polemical reasons, I believe. Before him Bergson had taken a position exactly opposite to that of Auguste Comte, and, since Bachelard in turn took the exact opposite position as Bergson, he found himself back in the company of Auguste Comte, without realizing it. In this way positivism, behind restored facades, has not budged an inch in its teaching or in its position in academia.

Now then, in rereading him in detail, I found Auguste Comte to be more profound than his successors, first as the inventor of sociology, and for having been the first to ask the question about the relations between science and society, and, more important, between the histories of science and religion. In this he remains unequaled; none of his successors, in any language, go as far on this decisive point.

The long work I put into the scientific editing of Comte's *Cours de philosophie positive,* published in 1975 by Hermann [*The Positive Philosophy*], taught me a lot. I do not regret the years spent in searching out the sources in Laplace, Lagrange, Fourier, Monge, or Carnot . . . and in reversing the popular idea people had of Comte, which often came from quoting him without reading him. He was conservative, often in the wrong in his epistemological evaluations of the science of his day—sometimes so totally wrong that one has only to turn him around, compass reading by compass reading, in order to discover, through symmetry, the sciences of the future. But he was a genius—the word is not too strong—in his apprehension of social and religious life, at the end of his life, when everyone thought he was crazy. This is a part of his work that is undeservedly ignored.

To return to Bachelard, he consummated the rupture that we've talked about between science and the humanities—perceiving on one side a spirit of burning the midnight oil and working and, on the other, a material imagination that sleeps, dreams, and ponders. This is a traditional and definitive way to bury the humanities in the sleep of reason, to submerge them, to identify them as lightweight, to burn them. It's an ethical, even moralistic, way of distinguishing: nocturnal laziness on one side, lucid activity on the other.

So, there exists no reasoned activity nor any valid ethics outside of the sciences. The Age of Enlightenment, by exalting scientific rationality, produced the Romantic Sturm und Drang, which took refuge in a literature of dreams and fog. Nothing new is born from this symmetry.

No matter how beautifully poetry sings, it remains imaginary and material—this is the theory of a two-pronged culture, which quickly struck me as scholastic and dangerous. On the contrary, the poems of La Fontaine, Verlaine, or Mallarmé require as much rigor as a geometric theorem, and a demonstration of the latter can sometimes deploy as much beauty as those poems themselves.

So, it was worthwhile to reflect on this common rigor and beauty, on this obviously single culture. We have neither two brains nor two bodies nor two souls.

BL I understand that you are forced, technically, to be at odds with Bachelard. He makes the precise rupture that you don't want to make. He is schizophrenic and proud of it.

MS No doubt. But I have never understood why one must be at odds, as you say, with those who do not share one's point of view. I feel and practice a good deal of friendship for people who are not of my opinion and whose disagreement teaches me more than others! Would we be in dialogue, either of us, without such a bond and a few opposite views?

BL You and Bachelard both maximize your differences.

MS Perhaps.

BL But what about your other colleagues in the history of science? For there was a different tradition. Duhem, for example . . .

MS Abandoned for a long time now, unfortunately—he was not much read and was scorned. The wars of religion at the beginning of this century in France finished him off. What a surprise for me to arrive in the United States a few years later and discover that there he still held a place of honor.

BL Forgotten by the historians?

MS By French-speaking historians of science. This is a particular case of a general law that in this country has few exceptions: in France you will always find a polemic whose arguments censure, at some point, one or another of our writers. Thus, we forget almost all of them, in our love for civil war on all subjects. We are producers of philosophy, but we teach as most important those of our neighbors. The most ignored authors in France are those writing in the French language. Likewise, according to the polls, the musicians least listened to are our own, and so forth.

We don't have an official censorship committee, but our civil wars effectively replace it. As you may have guessed, my great enterprise of publishing the "Corpus des oeuvres de philosophie en langue française" (soon to reach one hundred volumes) is done in a spirit of pacifism. In it I have republished Pierre Duhem, in fact, and a lot of others who had been buried by petty squabbles—atheists and abbots, left-wingers and right-wingers, politicians and scientists, rich men and paupers, men and women—who would not listen to one another. The dynamic of exclusion quickly produces a vacuum.

BL So, writing the history of science could be a peacemaking enterprise?

MS In it one is forced to connect the sciences to one another, and to other cultural formations. Let's give Husserl his due—his *Krisis* invents precisely this notion of cultural formation. In his description of the crisis in Western science he wonders if this original formation that we call science is independent of the others. This word *formation,* as he uses it, signifies something like a layer of the

Earth, geologically formed and deformed by and through the Earth's evolution. The problem is well put.

BL So, when you make the history of science into a trade (for lack of a more exalted designation), you don't separate science from the rest of culture, as nearly everyone else does, but seek to rebuild the links between internalism and externalism, as they say?

MS Since at the Ecole Normale I had worked on the structures of modern algebra, it remained for me to do the same work on topology, and I had begun it. The latter fascinates me, even much more than the former. I encountered Leibniz while tracing the histories of these two disciplines, since it can be said that he practically invented both of them, including their contemporary guises. At that time he dazzled me as an inspired anticipator of our era— even in communication technology, in logic, in relativity. But in order to study Leibniz it's not enough to know mathematics or science in general; one must become the historian of these, must learn the Latin of that era, etc.

Now, the history of science had little to do with Greco-Latin culture. The split occurred there, too. If good antiquarians or excellent medievalists study Leibniz, they know nothing of his scientific writings. Likewise, historians of the sciences do not take into account the *Theodicy*. Here I must plead guilty, because it wasn't until I read Christiane Frémont that I realized that my Leibniz, although systematic, was incomplete. In my preface to her book on the correspondence with Barthelemy des Bosses, *L'Etre et la relation,* I admitted that I had been wrong—by default, precisely.

I was teaching at Clermont-Ferrand when I wrote this first book, and I remember the decision made by some administrator or cabinet minister to separate the libraries of science and of letters. How could you tear apart the very pages of Leibniz, Pascal, Plato, Aristotle, Diderot, Lewis Carroll, and so many others? What's more—luckily or unluckily—scientists themselves rarely consider as "science" the texts published earlier than the generation preceding their own.

BL So, for you the important problem was never the relationship between science and philosophy but, rather, the problem between philosophy and the humanities, which remains the most impoverished point of all?

MS What philosophy worthy of the name has truly been able to avoid the link between poem and theorem?

BL But there still were historians of science. You had colleagues. Did you ever take pleasure in your profession?

MS Sometimes. Not often.

BL Even back then?

MS Great professional misfortunes befell me, which I don't like to talk about, because it has taken me a very long time to recover from them. In short, I had to teach the history of science, but in a department of history—I was distanced, excluded, expelled forever from teaching philosophy. I suffered a lot over it, and no doubt I still suffer from it. I was thus deprived of any professional milieu—students and colleagues—which is a hard way to live, and I was again left in solitude. I only found true collaborators at one or two generations' remove, when you and I and some talented young people published our *Eléments d'histoire des sciences,* but that was in 1989, more than twenty years later. A thanks, in passing, to those who agreed to work with me.

BL As far as you are concerned, this was an accident?

MS A tragedy, a punishment—how can I tell? In any case, a definitive isolation.

BL Nonetheless, just plain history—that of Braudel and the Annales— *was considered to be in full renewal in the glorious sixties. It didn't interest you?*

MS No doubt it was my own fault. I was never a good historian, because I never can understand which *time,* singular or plural, is in question in history. Moreover, history is able to talk about everything without being falsifiable. I, too, have worked all my life on these subjects. No doubt I will only ever be worthy of teaching historians when I am verging on retirement. I have been working for a long time on a book on time and history. It advances as slowly as my own intuition on these two matters.

The Futility of Discussion

BL What is hardest for me to understand, perhaps because I belong more to the Anglo-Saxon world, is your relationship to discussion. You never see it as anything but a dispute. For you the intellectual milieu is always one of warfare with each and all. Nonetheless, you have had colleagues who have influenced you. Was it much later that you knew René Girard?

MS Yes, much later, when I taught at Johns Hopkins in Baltimore and in Buffalo, New York, and at Stanford, in California. He had an influence on me similar to what I'd received from Simone Weil. He also had read *Gravity and Grace* in his youth, and he freely admits that his thoughts on violence were born from meditating on Simone Weil's texts.

BL But what about anthropologists like Claude Lévi-Strauss or mythologists like Georges Dumézil?

MS Until very recently, in order to get a teaching credential in philosophy, you had to have earned a certificate in one of the sciences, chosen from a list that included mathematics, physics, chemistry, biology—in short, the hard or fairly hard sciences—and ethnology or prehistory, what we might call the softer or more human sciences. Those students of philosophy with no scientific training always chose to take the exam in ethnology or prehistory. This is the reason for philosophers' sudden interest—the fad even—for the so-called human, or social, sciences. You are right: great intellectual movements can often be explained by reasons springing from the sociology of science; one has only to invent an entrance exam, and the corresponding science will exist.

In short, since I already had a degree in mathematics, I didn't need to study the softer sciences, so I missed out on that movement, and on its major works, but I know structuralism very well, since it was algebraic in origin. You can imagine my surprise back then when I learned that there was a linguistic structuralism. But mine came more from Bourbaki, from algebraic or topologic structures. And it is somewhat different, it seems to me. The passage of time has confirmed in me the idea that this structuralism must be the true one.

BL But how did you meet people like Dumézil?

MS It seemed to me that he applied an authentic structuralism to the humanities, to religious history—a discipline that has always fascinated me, since I am still convinced that it forms the deepest plate in the history of cultures. By *plate* I mean what earth scientists mean by this word—thus continuing the image Husserl used when he spoke of "formation." A plate that is deeply submerged, buried, often opaque and dark, that transforms itself with infinite slowness but which explains very well the discontinuous changes and perceptible ruptures that take place above. Indeed, in comparison to religious history, that of the sciences seems superficial, recent—like a surface landscape, quite visible and shimmering. What's more, when you study religious history in detail, that of the sciences seems to imitate or repeat it!

I only knew Dumézil too late, unfortunately. Foucault introduced me to him. I felt closer to Dumézil than to Lévi-Strauss, simply because the former had a Greco-Latin, Indo-European basis for his research, which was familiar to me, while I never had any kind of mastery over Native American mythology. With the one I could verify; with the other I could not.

BL Speaking of Foucault, what were your relations with him?

MS Pupil and colleague.

BL Pupil at the Ecole Normale?

MS Right. I need to answer you now about discussion and its fruitfulness. I'm not convinced that debate ever advances thinking. Let's take as an example the debate on chance and determinism that created quite a stir in the press a while back. All of its argumentation repeats, point by point and without notable variation, the debate that created a big stir in the Stalinist era, on Heisenberg's indeterminism. The same camps, the same divisions, the same punches. And this argumentation itself repeated exactly the antitheses and condemnations so amiably exchanged between the strict positivists of the nineteenth century, in the style of Auguste Comte, and the adherents of Laplace. These arguments figure prominently in Comte's *The Positive Philosophy.* One can thus go back to the classical age of Pascal and the Bernoullis, to the invention of calculating probabilities.

Don't you think you're wasting your time when you engage in such a polemic? Since war is the most common thing in the world, it causes the indefinite repetition of the same gestures and the same ideas. Neither debate nor criticism makes any advances, except on the social chessboard and in the conquest of power. By what strange aberration were they believed to be fruitful, since they kill?

What makes for advancement in philosophy, and also in science, is inventing concepts, and this invention always takes place in solitude, independence, and freedom—indeed, in silence. We have a surfeit of colloquia these days; what comes out of them? Collective repetitions. On the other hand, we are cruelly deprived of convents and quiet cells and the taciturn rules of the cenobites and anchorites.

Debate brings pressure to bear, which always tends to confirm accepted ideas. It exacerbates them, vitrifies them, constructs and closes off lobbying groups. At the very most it sometimes chisels out clarifications, but it never makes discoveries. But unless philosophy is devoted to commentary, it ridicules retracing existing concepts.

Discussion conserves; invention requires rapid intuition and being as light as weightlessness.

BL Since I don't share your experience of debate and of group work, I will keep asking about your entourage! Even though Foucault was a faithful pupil of Canguilhem, wasn't he in a sense making in the social sciences the same link as you between society, knowledge, and power?

MS After being his pupil, I was his colleague for several years at Vincennes (University of Paris VIII), but first at Clermont-Ferrand. There we discussed *Les Mots et les choses [The Order of Things]* every week while he was working on it. A large part of this book was written after discussions between us. But it was not a debate—far from it. At that time both of us were living on the fringes. The structuralist aspect that has been attributed to this work comes from this close collaboration.

BL This great project of Foucault's could have had many more links with yours. It addressed the problem of the emergence of the social sciences, of structures and formations . . .

MS He was playing the social science score, and I was playing the score of natural science, so we could collaborate without difficulty. We never had any trouble working together on methodology. I had already written an article on his *Histoire de la folie [Madness and Civilization]*, reprinted in my first *Hermes* book, in which I tried to trace geometric structures. But later, after *Surveiller et punir [Discipline and Punish]*, I no longer followed him. We lost track of each other after an unavowed political disagreement—no, it was more about the ethics of teaching—at Vincennes. I always was very fond of him. He continued the great French university tradition, following in the footsteps of Hazard and Brunschvicg. The latter had written the historico-philosophical panorama of mathematics and then of physics; *The Order of Things* did the same thing for the human sciences.

BL What about projects like Derrida's, for the humanities?

MS I never participated in the Heideggerian tradition. I only read his *Being and Time* much later. I've already said why.

BL This negative experience of discussions, do you hold to it?

MS Why get into discussions of determinism and chaos, when the same things have been said, by the same factions, in nearly every generation? No, debate is not productive. This is why a few years ago I sent to a journal organizing an issue on Balzac a pastiche of Balzac on *La Belle Noiseuse,* in which chaos takes her oldest name, *Noise.* Yes, chaos itself is interesting—I even believe I was the first philosopher to speak about it—but discussion is not interesting; it is so repetitive.

Polemic never invents anything, because nothing is older, anthropologically, than war. The opposite notion has become conventional wisdom in the Anglo-Saxon world, which today holds sway. It is because it holds sway that this method is propagated. That's always the strategy of victors. Reread Plato: Socrates always imposes the methodology by which he always wins. Dialectics is the logic of the masters. It's necessary first of all to impose, in a manner defying discussion, the methodology for discussion.

BL I don't agree, since I myself have only had positive experiences of discussion, in a group of colleagues, but it's unimportant. Our readers are going to have the following problem: everyone considers the 1950s and 1960s as a great period . . .

MS As Aesop said, the best and the worst.

BL *. . . a great period for the French intelligentsia, with Lévi-Strauss, Foucault, Sartre, the great disputes. Everyone misses that eminent period in philosophy, when methodology was being invented, precisely, in the social sciences, in anthropology. . . . It's considered to have been a great period, and, furthermore, for a long time you were placed in the structuralist movement.*

MS We're jumping ahead in time to the 1960s—we'll talk about it later. The worst and the best had taken place in France—the worst, because a sort of glaciation affected intellectual and university life, through terror, conformism, and repression. But in the final assessment you are right; on the balance sheet of those years France was one of the rare countries to see an intellectual renaissance.

But did those who didn't choose the superhighways really contribute something new? Like Gilles Deleuze, for example. He separated himself from the traditional history of philosophy, from the human sciences, from epistemology. He's an excellent example of the dynamic movement of free and inventive thinking.

BL *Dumézil too. He had a completely atypical career.*

MS Dumézil was ridiculed by all of his colleagues, all his life. Even at the Collège de France and at the French Academy he was considered not only as atypical but often as eccentric, like Bergson, who also did not have the good fortune of pleasing his university colleagues. Was Bergson ever discussed? Can an intuition be discussed? Aren't the great inventions, including the conceptual ones, based on an intuition? It always makes the first move; the rank and file discuss afterward, to tear one another apart.

BL *But I see this completely social trait from the outside, and I don't much believe in it. All the great French intellectuals claim to be persecuted. Foucault like the rest. Bourdieu is at the Collège de France, he's an advisor to cabinet ministers, and he believes he's a pariah. Derrida thinks he's persecuted. Isn't this a French trait? Each one of them claims that the other has the positions of power and that he alone is engaged in mortal combat against universal opposition.*

MS You may be right. But twenty-five years of teaching in the United States have not persuaded me that there is better mental health on that side of the Atlantic than on this one. Resentment is the daily bread of an underpaid profession, now fallen below the poverty line. The university itself must produce such temperaments—wasn't it already the case in the Middle Ages?

Let's talk more about Gilles Deleuze, who was truly and seriously exiled from academic circles. The greatest praise I can say of him is that philosophy made him truly happy. Profoundly serene. And thus, once again, exemplary.

BL You have taught for a large part of your life in the United States. Do you generalize your negative experience of discussion to that country as well?

MS The greatest difference between France and the Anglo-Saxon countries, which you invoke, comes neither from ethics or psychopathology, nor from academic practices, I believe, but from the political system. Here we live in a republic, and they have established a democracy. That has profound repercussions for intellectual and everyday life.

The republic, built on a collective and theoretical ideal, in practice allows us to live and think as separate individuals and as unique in type—which is the reason for the solitude I speak of, and for the perpetual squabbles that, unfortunately, often degenerate into true civil wars. This is also the reason for the devastating criticism the French exercise on the collectivity in which they live. They can never find words harsh enough to attack what goes on in France, including culture.

On the other hand, Anglo-Saxon democracy requires, in practice, that each person unflaggingly construct an egalitarian collectivity, as durable as possible, which forces people into conformity, as one quickly notices there. This is the reason for the relative peace at the very heart of debate, which you advocate, and for the praise, for the permanent PR they indulge in about the collectivity in which they live.

If you now put in competition our system of self-criticism and this other one of self-promotion, guess which one will win out, at least in discussions and in the media? Nonetheless, I believe that the system we call a republic, in spite of current prevailing opinion, is much more advanced.

So, as far as intellectual life and invention are concerned, for science, as a collectivity, it is perhaps better to have democracy, which produces the contract of conformity. But for a creative work, which is far more personal, the republic wins hands down, since it exacerbates individualism. This is how I would resolve the problem that you pose in terms of persecution or mental illness. Political sociology, in which you excel more than I, actually does have something to offer sometimes.

But to finish up on the methodology of discussion, for me it was perhaps the experience of the war that irrevocably cut that thread. Sartre's dominant position no doubt also has something to do with it. He crushes everything and understands nothing. Through his ignorance of the sciences and their formidable reverberations in society, he delayed the arrival of all the real innovations. And at a certain point his ethic of "commitment" becomes the required ethic, sterilizing invention, which is always solitary.

And what if, apropos of debate, we were to finish this conversation as we began it—with war? You are of a certain age and take your inspiration from a country that likes debate and war, assured as they are of winning—through science and power—except for a few truck accidents. On the other hand, I am of a certain age and I am a descendant of cultures, languages, and countries too weak, ignorant, and poor not to lose those wars and debates. Do you believe that those who bury the dead and mourn before the silence and indifference of the powerful—do you believe that the hundreds of thousands of dead—believe in the fruitfulness of battles and in the advancement of history through slaughter?

BL So, in a nutshell, your formation would be this: in search of the solitary state?

MS The formation of a philosopher necessarily lasts a long time. Through the vicissitudes of history and vocational misfortunes mine was also austere and painful. It took me decades to free myself from this first powerful influence—misery and death as a daily condition, three cents and life as rare and exceptional. Finally, as a reaction and a resurrection, or through nature, need, or necessity, I drew from it an irrepressible love for life, an inexpressible and continuous pleasure in at least existing, and in contemplating, when I have occasion to do so.

Through family tradition I seemed more destined for fairly servile, manual labor. And because my youth was contemporary to so many wars, I seemed more destined to negative emotions and thoughts. But in both cases I found myself completely on the other side of things. Indeed, I only love positive values, and I feel an irrepressible happiness in practicing my chosen vocation, in teaching (I love my students) and in writing books (if necessary, I would pay to do it). Enthusiasm for the philosophical life has never left me. If I had to name (perhaps immodestly) the dominant sentiment that is always with me, I would not hesitate a moment: joy, the immense, sparkling, indeed holy joy of having to think—a joy that is sometimes even serenity.

BL So, the somber character of your formation hasn't marked your work with tragedy?

MS When a person's life begins with the experience and atmosphere of death, it can only move forward in an ongoing spirit of birth, of rebirth, of a positive and overflowing wellspring of exhilaration. Whom do I thank for having rescued me from all that, for having had such luck? After that dark tableau of history I must exalt the magnificence of an existence dedicated, minute by minute, in great enthusiasm, to a life's work whose value I no doubt will never truly know—a dubitative and fragile marvel.

Method

Bruno Latour: In our last session we talked about your formation—about what had happened to you. Your books are difficult to read because you do not affiliate yourself with any precise tradition. You have "neither masters nor disciples." You described to us the historical and intellectual situations that had made you "gun-shy," wounded by an era that in your experience was not a glorious one. You have removed one of the great difficulties encountered by me and your readers—at least your uninitiated readers. Your triple affirmation of the sciences, philosophy, and literature explains why intellectual debates interest you so little. While not fully explained, your idiosyncrasy is becoming clearer.

Michel Serres: Freedom of thought always has to be reinvented. Unfortunately, thought is usually only found constrained and forced, in a context rigid with impossibilities. To refer again to the memories evoked earlier (with neither pleasure nor indulgence), I would sum them up as a set of formidable barriers confronting an almost savage need for freedom. I needed to escape at all costs from that.

BL That's precisely what I wanted to talk about today. For your readers and for me this freedom of thought is translated by a second great difficulty. It's no longer: "Where is this guy coming from? Why doesn't he take his place in a tradition?" We've dealt with that problem. Rather, it's: "How does he proceed? How does he get from point to point?" Why, in the space of one paragraph, do we find ourselves with the Romans then with Jules Verne then with the Indo-Europeans then, suddenly, launched in the Chal-lenger rocket, before ending up on a bank of the Garonne River? We can see your footprints here and there, but we don't see the path that links them. One has the impression that you have a time machine that gives you this amazing freedom of movement. But we, as pedestrians, don't see it, and we say to ourselves, "There's got to be a trick here somewhere."

MS In the comparative disciplines you can find yourself in ancient Rome then poof! in Ireland and Wales then, without a pause, poof! in Vedic India. Have you asked Georges Dumézil this question? With the encyclopedic philosophers—Aristotle, Leibniz, Auguste Comte—there you are among the animals and then, poof! in politics and then, without warning, among theorems. Have you asked this question of Kant, who passes from astronomy to law to geography and anthropology before writing his *Critiques?*

BL I'm pointing out the difficulties to you so that you can explain them away. This time machine, this freedom of movement, is at the bottom of the accusations of "poetry" leveled at your books, harmful accusations that I know exasperate you . . .

MS What a sign of the times, when, to cruelly criticize a book, one says that it is only poetry! *Poetry* comes from the Greek, meaning "invention," "creation"—so all is well, thank you.

BL I wanted to talk about that. Your books are technical, your arguments are concise, your demonstrations precise. But when a reader likes Serres, he says, "It's beautiful—I didn't understand it—it's poetry." And when a reader doesn't like him, he says simply, "It's poetry." I think if you could spend a few minutes showing me your time machine—your flying saucer— from behind the scenes, I would understand better.

MS How shall we begin?

All Authors Are Our Contemporaries

BL With time. I think your most striking trait for all of us, as modern readers, is that you are absolutely indifferent to temporal distances. For you Pythagoras and Lucretius are no more or less distant than La Fontaine or Brillouin. One would say that for you there is no such thing as time. That everything is contemporary. But we, as pedestrians, say: "Neverthe-less, Livy is way back there and buried. How can he mix him in with contemporary science?" What enables you to bring together in the same

*time frame all these genres, authors, books, myths? We'll talk later about
what makes the links among them.*

MS In order to say "contemporary," one must already be thinking
of a certain time and thinking of it in a certain way. Do you
remember what we said earlier about historians' "time"? So, let's
put the question differently: What things are contemporary? Consider a late-model car. It is a disparate aggregate of scientific and
technical solutions dating from different periods. One can date it
component by component: this part was invented at the turn of
the century, another, ten years ago, and Carnot's cycle is almost
two hundred years old. Not to mention that the wheel dates back
to neolithic times. The ensemble is only contemporary by assemblage, by its design, its finish, sometimes only by the slickness of
the advertising surrounding it.

Likewise, how many books appearing today are really and entirely contemporary? Take, for example, some book that seeks to
reflect on certain recent scientific discoveries. Its philosophical
reflection dates from the eighteenth century and earlier—a sort
of scientistic materialism in the style of Helvétius or Holbach.
There is often a serious lag between philosophical debate and
scientific information. While the latter dates from today, the philosophical reflections that the author draws from it come from a
bygone era, and this discrepancy makes these books—and certain
debates, as I have already noted—into veritable caricatures.

This is often the case in epistemology. The two elements rarely
date from the same period. It's like a building with one Greek
wing, complete with columns and pediment, and the other, contemporary, pre-formed concrete and tinted glass. Half–Mona Lisa,
half–Max Ernst. Come on now—do you split atoms with a pickax?
When I began my studies I even had the impression that there was
no truly *contemporary* reflection on the sciences.

BL Wasn't there?

MS Not that I know of. Even the analytical school is still and
endlessly refining questions already resolved or asked either in the
eighteenth century in French-language texts or in the Middle Ages
in universities using Latin or in Greek antiquity in the Sophist
schools. When philosophy is trapped and enclosed in academia it
doesn't move much. What continues perennially is the institution,

whose function remains the reproduction of obedient young people. One could say that it imposes a method.

On the other hand, the questions I encountered were new and pressing, truly unexpected, unforeseeable: never had science so imposed itself on humanity. It was imperative to promote a modernity.

BL I don't understand. You wanted to be modern?

MS What I am and *when* I am is not really important. But I want to be able to understand time and, in particular, *a self-same time.*

I will take another simple example. In rereading Lucretius' text, everyone says that the philosophical state of mechanistic materialism as discussed from antiquity to the nineteenth century is over. Experimental science has advanced from these abstract dreams, has uprooted itself from this discussion and made it definitively pointless. So, Perrin's *atoms* no longer have anything to do with Lucretius' *elements.* Thus, the latter is no longer contemporary or even readable at all; he belongs to the Latin scholars, on the one hand, and to the historians of materialism, on the other. In this way he is twice lost—so why study him in philosophy? Besides, "it's poetry."

But, in carefully rereading the *De rerum natura,* I see that in reality he's talking about fluid mechanics, about turbulence and chaos, that he's asking—and asking well—questions about chance and determinism, that his *clinamen,* a first curvature, is also a breaking of symmetry. I see that one could not read these things as long as the science of the day obliged one to think exclusively in terms of the mechanics of solids, that the mathematics he calls upon are precisely those of Archimedes, that thus he is uninfluenced by Epicurus and Euclid. Indeed, here he is truly contemporary, not only in his scientific content but in his philosophic reflection. Even more contemporary because he is passionately interested in questions of violence, in the relations between religion and science, and, so, suddenly very much more up-to-date than the horrible mass of books that claim to be the latest word on these problems, in a vocabulary that is conscientiously "contemporary."

BL Wait a minute. What meaning do you give to the word contemporary?

MS The word *contemporary* automatically takes two contradictory meanings. It means that Lucretius, *in his own time,* really was already thinking in terms of flux, turbulence, and chaos, and, second, that *through this, he is part of our era,* which is rethinking similar problems. I must change time frames and no longer use the one that history uses.

Just yesterday I attended a debate on Lucretius at the Centre National de la Recherche Scientifique, where Latin scholars and atomic scientists could not hear themselves talk, with the same schizophrenia as always. On the one hand, those who studied the Latin text—literary critics and philosophers—held forth either on dialectical materialism or on Lucretius' anguish, his heartbreaks, and, on the other hand, the scientists repeated their neutral discourse, launched into orbit without any relation to these soulful matters. Each person was sealed off in his own time.

To reread Lucretius as I have done gives him back both his own Latin quality and this double contemporaneity. Mediterranean antiquity had water shortages and, thus, thought only of fluids, and our science has long since advanced beyond the exclusive, mechanistic consideration of solids. Some amazing connections ensue. Thus, although I seem to you to be situated outside of time, in a sort of formidable contemporaneity, making a dazzling shortcut between poetic and scientific temporality, I am actually restoring the true meaning—double and unique—both of tradition and of today's science.

In what temporality is the scholasticism of the text imprisoned? The bifurcated relationship between science and literature was so frozen, so distant, that two eternities seemed to be looking at each other like two porcelain dogs—like two stone lions flanking a doorway.

BL That's a perfect caricature.

MS This caricature is omnipresent and makes the usual way of studying Lucretius and so many others positively unbearable. It is both stupid from the point of view of the Latin (I found so many reversals of meaning in the standard translation!) and absurd from the point of view of science. I have used a technique of rapprochement that brings things really back to our time.

The Past Is No Longer Out-of-Date

BL You're going too fast. This problem of time is the greatest source of incomprehension, in my opinion. What makes other people's "past" empty, frozen, nontemporal, is the supposition that the past is out-of-date.

MS An excellent way of putting it. In former times this was called a rupture—there is a chasm between Lucretius' atoms and those of Perrin, between mythic antiquity and contemporary science, which makes the past bygone and the present authentic. This thesis has always seemed to me quasi-religious: it supposes that between long-lost times and the new era there is some advent, some birth of a new time.

BL Are you saying that the rationalist idea of epistemological ruptures is itself an archaic idea?

MS Let me say a word on the idea of progress. We conceive of time as an irreversible line, whether interrupted or continuous, of acquisitions and inventions. We go from generalizations to discoveries, leaving behind us a trail of errors finally corrected—like a cloud of ink from a squid. "Whew! We've finally arrived at the truth." It can never be demonstrated whether this idea of time is true or false.

But, irresistibly, I cannot help thinking that this idea is the equivalent of those ancient diagrams we laugh at today, which place the Earth at the center of everything, or our galaxy at the middle of the universe, to satisfy our narcissism. Just as in space we situate ourselves at the center, at the navel of the things in the universe, so for time, through progress, we never cease to be at the summit, on the cutting edge, at the state-of-the-art of development. It follows that we are always right, for the simple, banal, and naive reason that we are living in the present moment. The curve traced by the idea of progress thus seems to me to sketch or project into time the vanity and fatuousness expressed spatially by that central position. Instead of inhabiting the heart or the middle of the world, we are sojourning at the summit, the height, the best of truth.

This diagram allows us permanently (yes, *permanently,* since the present is always the last word on time and truth; "permanently"— that's a good paradox for a theory of historical evolution) to be not only right but to be righter than was ever possible before. Now I believe that one should always be wary of any person or theory that is always right: he's not plausible; it's not probable.

BL For me, for an ordinary reader, what makes your demonstration unbe-lievable—improbable—is that you can't treat Lucretius as a contemporary, because his science is obviously obsolete. And it's the scientists, the episte-mologists, who constantly argue that there is no scientific thought before themselves.

MS Scientists often think like Descartes: "No one has thought before me." This Descartes-effect produces good publicity, very effective and convincing: "No one ever thought such-and-such un-til I said it." This boast contradicts the *Philosophia perennis* and is totally absurd.

BL It's this kind of philosophy that makes the past totally distant. It's obvious to us moderns that, as we advance in time, each successive stage outstrips the preceding one.

MS But that's not *time.*

BL That's what you need to explain to me—why this passage of time is not time.

MS That's not time, only a simple line. It's not even a line, but a trajectory of the race for first place—in school, in the Olympic Games, for the Nobel Prize. This isn't time, but a simple competi-tion—once again, war. Why replace temporality, duration, with a quarrel? *The first to arrive, the winner of the battle, obtains as his prize the right to reinvent history to his own advantage.* Once again dialec-tics—which is nothing more than the logic of appearances.

More profoundly, time alone can make co-possible two contra-dictory things. As an example, I am young and old. Only my life, its time or its duration, can make these two propositions coherent between themselves. Hegel's error was in reversing this logical evidence and in claiming that contradiction produces time, whereas only the opposite is true: time makes contradiction possible. This error is the source of all the absurdities recounted since then on war, "the mother of history."

No, war is mother only to death, first of all, and then perpetually to war. It gives birth only to nothingness and, identically, to itself. So, destruction repeats itself, which is the reason for the eternal return of debate. History fairly regularly vindicates those who don't believe in such Hegelian schemas.

The hypothesis that before a given generation there was no science denies all temporality, all history. On the other hand, tradition often gives us ideas still filled with vitality.

BL Excuse me, but where do you get this idea from?

MS Can I return to my training? I earned a degree in classical studies, in Latin and Greek, and I was also trained in science, earning two degrees in mathematics. Through my entire life I have never abandoned this double route. I still read Plutarch and the great physicists, at the same time, as a refusal of the separation between science and literature, of this divorce that informs the temporality of so-called contemporary thought.

BL This same separation? The separation between literature and science?

MS Yes. The Age of Enlightenment was very instrumental in categorizing as irrational any reason not formed by science. Now, I maintain that there is as much reason in the works of Montaigne or Verlaine as there is in physics or biochemistry and, reciprocally, that often there is as much unreason scattered through the sciences as there is in certain dreams. Reason is statistically distributed everywhere; no one can claim exclusive rights to it.

This division thus is echoed in the image, in the imaginary picture that one makes of time. Instead of condemning or excluding, one consigns a certain thing to antiquity, to archaism. One no longer says "false" but, rather, "out-of-date," or "obsolete." In earlier times people dreamed; now we think. Once people sang poetry; today we experiment efficiently. History is thus the projection of this very real exclusion into an imaginary, even imperialistic time. The temporal rupture is the equivalent of a dogmatic expulsion.

On the one hand, there's the gradual disappearance of great authors—those whose ancient culture refers to the archaic age of poetry, which no one needs. On the other hand, scientists, as the only "contemporaries," speak the truth about the world or the brain, math or physics. Since you know the United States well, you know with what delight it consigns Europe to Pompeii or the era of the great cathedrals. It's an excellent way of saying, "Today, we are advancing while you are in charge of the museums." History lends a certain impression of reality to self-promotion.

Scientists at the beginning of this century didn't yet feel this divorce. Jean Perrin, in *Les Atomes,* cites Lucretius from the beginning and even performs anew experiments and observations inspired by the Latin text. In his study you'll find an annotated copy of Lucretius. Another example: at the beginning of his *Celestial Mechanics* Laplace passes in review all the mechanists who preceded him, starting with the ancient Greeks.

BL Now you're introducing another confusion. In the case of Laplace or Perrin it's a recapitulation, demonstrating the growth of reason. All scientists can sketch out a brief history in which they place themselves at the pinnacle of reason, after centuries of groping.

MS That's right—you're correct—and I am saying the same thing.

BL If I understand correctly, your own way of showing the past has nothing to do with the growth of reason?

MS No.

BL What is the articulation between the distinction, on the one hand, of the sciences from the humanities and, on the other, of the out-of-date or long-lost past from the uniquely rational present?

MS That took place in the eighteenth century, which sought to remove all rationality from anything that was not science: it's science's bid to take over the totality of reason. Those areas suddenly bereft of reason include religion, of course, literature and the humanities, as well as history and the past: they are all consigned to the irrational. And the nineteenth century of Sturm und Drang will confirm this momentous decision by confining all literary movements to myths and dreams. In this regard, the history of science, epistemology, scientists, and even the man in the street went along with this idea, which is the source of the usual historical diagram: reason later, unreason before. What can we call this, except prejudice?

The converse prejudice is no more enlightening, though—claiming that we have totally forgotten an initial intuition received and developed only by certain pre-Socratics, among the ancient Greeks. This intuition emanates, of course, from the greatest denigrators of science and technology. So, we have a nice symmetry, like the two lions we were speaking of earlier!

If the redoubtable problem of historical time could be resolved so simply, we would know about it.

BL But you, you claim that, as the saying goes, those who ignore history are condemned to repeat—on the contrary—out-of-date arguments and philosophical movements.

MS Yes.

BL So, you want to escape from both of these?

MS To ignore the past is often to run the risk of repeating it. How many times have we read a book intoxicated with recent invention, whose author boasts of having finally escaped from certain ideas and ways of feeling and perceiving, which he innocently repeats without realizing it! We could name ten examples.

Neither Judgment nor Absence of Judgment

BL Having said this, there is a problem. Your argument completely contradicts the most fundamental thesis of Bachelard's and Canguilhem's philosophy of the official sciences, embraced in France, at least, by all scientists. The distinction Canguilhem makes between history and epistemology is clear. History collects facts, even if they are false. Epistemology has the task of judging, of outlawing the false and only keeping the true. Your definition of the passage of time no longer has any rapport with the dogma of French epistemology.

MS Let's remain fair: Canguilhem wrote an excellent article on Auguste Comte, in which he praises him for not deprecating things from an earlier era—from the age of superstition.

Since I had abandoned epistemology, I also dropped any judgmental perspective. Criticism is never fertile, and evaluation of the sciences is not even possible, since they fluctuate so rapidly. Although it is valued in academia, criticism is easy, temporary, fugitive, quickly out of style. If yesterday's truth is tomorrow's error, then in the sciences it likewise happens that the error condemned today will sooner or later find itself in the treasure house of great discoveries.

Furthermore, it is stimulating to restore to material judged irrational the respect owed to straight reason, even if it means redefining the latter. For example, finding an authentic science in Lucretius, in authors, poets, novelists, or theologians—thousands of whom used to call themselves rational.

BL So, we should abandon both the belief that they are out-of-date and the possibility of judging them on the basis of the current state of science?

MS The so-called current state of science. Who can affirm that this is really contemporary, except the inventors, who are present and active in the forefront of discovery? This question and the immense difficulty in answering it make what Sartre called "commitment" very problematical. Who is truly of our era, can you tell me?

BL But to say this is to abandon the idea that, by being ignorant of certain arguments, we will repeat even older ones.

MS True.

BL But to do that is completely to realign eras.

MS In the end we'd almost have to speak of uneducating. As soon as you bring together on an island all those who are right and who assume the right to judge everything and you abandon everything else, by ignoring this *everything else,* you run the risk of repeating it. To forget exposes one to repeating.

BL So, your own principle of movement . . .

MS . . . is to struggle against forgetting. As a result, your reproach to me about ignoring history is reversed; in other words, who really speaks about history?

BL Yes, but now we run into another difficulty: your history is not Bachelardian, in the sense that it is not the sanctioned history.

MS No, since I suspend all judgment. Have you noticed that the term *sanctioned* comes both from the law and from religion, to reaffirm *sanctified?*

BL But, furthermore, your history is not historicist, in the sense that you don't want to go and recover history as it was for the people of the period. That doesn't interest you either. You want neither the sanctioned history of the epistemologists nor the dated, historicist, documentary history of the historians. Is it because you want this bygone history to live again now?

MS Yes. To take up again the example of Lucretius, contemporary physics at least allows us to reread him, but in an oblique manner, and finally to discover some actuality that is still active. What do we mean by oblique here? That if you translate atom by atom, you will not get very far. You must look somewhat alongside, or more globally, at the system of turbulence. In the last century William Thomson still was assimilating atoms to vortices in fluids, so the tradition I am reviving dates from two thousand years ago and has been forgotten for scarcely a hundred years. It doesn't necessarily come to us from remote antiquity. Sometimes things that seem to have been forgotten for a long time are actually conserved quite close to us. Which is the reason for the time lapse I'm talking about.

Even the best disciples of Descartes have forgotten their master on this point: he is much more the forerunner of contemporary physics than Newton, who only yesterday was held by our predecessors to be more modern. Yes, vortices are pulling ahead of universal attraction, far from being reduced to a fiction of physics, as Leibniz said. The heavens of the galaxies, of meteorologists, even the space of particles are more and more Cartesian—sown by whirlwinds and turbulences.

BL Yes, but to say that this is a time that is still active—this is not a historian's position either. In none of your books do you attempt to "reconstitute the cultural environment of Lucretius," to "seek out the texts he might have read," and thereby utilize history to transport us from our era to that of the Romans.

MS No.

BL What always interests you is the reverse movement. To take Lucretius, to leap over the philosophers who discount him by saying he's obsolete, and to bring him to the hypotheses that are current in physics.

MS That's right. What's more, this is a way—a strategy, a ruse—to answer another question: that of loss. Everything has its price. As science advances, we rarely evaluate the substantial cultural losses that correspond to the gains. Literature becomes evanescent through a loss of substance, while, on the other hand, there is a considerable gain in scientific intelligence—in both content and institutions.

This is behind my temptation to write a defense and an illustration of the humanities—in the face of, in opposition to, and for the benefit of scientists themselves. To say to them: "Lucretius thinks more profoundly and even more rationally than many of today's scientists. A novelist like Zola invented thermodynamic operators well before the science of thermodynamics; he introduced them without even realizing it. Read this or that poem by Verlaine." I want to show a certain *reason* in its emerging state and illustrate it for the benefit of academic reason.

BL Yes, but with a double difficulty. You reuse authors and texts considered by the epistemologists to be proscribed and out-of-date.

MS "When you hear that Beethoven is out-of-date, listen to the music of those who make such claims," said Schumann with a smile. "Usually, they are nothing but composers of flat romances."

BL But at the same time, you aren't preserving texts on the same grounds as the humanities usually do—those of historicism.

MS Sometimes, not often.

BL You never say, "Let us respect them at least for their difference, for their eccentricity, as an interesting witness to bygone days." For you it's never a question of exoticism . . .

MS You're right.

BL . . . their past and their difference do not cancel out their effect of reality, of rationality. You don't respect their difference in the way that a historian or an ethnologist would. You place them on the same footing as the most modern theses.

MS Yes.

BL At the obvious risk . . .

MS . . . of not being heard by either the Latin scholar who has no use for hydrodynamics or the scientist who laughs at the *clinamen*. This defines the solitude of those who seek: it's not too serious;

what matters is what's correct. Who is not isolated, when he is seeking?

BL This is the problem we must address.

MS In fact, professional risk does exist. You have to accept paying its price—knowing that, on the one hand, humanists no longer recognize their customary Lucretius and that, on the other, scientists are totally uninterested in this story.

Except that this is starting to change. The theoreticians of turbulence are starting to say, "Yes, in fact, there is already in Lucretius this kind of thing." Except that each important discovery suddenly reveals an intelligent past behind a recent obstruction. With each new advance there is new amnesia! Each invention reveals both the real and the historical.

BL We'll come back to this point later. So, time experienced as present allows you to circumvent both those who claim that time is out-of-date and who are in fact immobile and those who say, "The only way to respect temporality is through the work of historians." This would define your enterprise.

MS It's almost a resurrection of dead texts. But since the university, through a maximal bifurcation, produces scientists, on the one hand, and purely literary scholars, on the other, messages destined for both parties are not well received.

BL Before we talk about that I want to make sure that I've rightly understood what you were saying—that the particular approach to time that interests you is the other side of the coin from the separation of the humanities and the sciences. This separation obliges the humanities to be historicist, to be content with the remains of the past, and to maximize their difference. The sciences are Bachelardian in their spontaneous philosophy—that is, they completely cancel out their past, in a sense from hour to hour, from year to year.

MS Yes.

BL So it's the same two-pronged problem: to settle the problem of time and to settle the problem of the sciences.

A Different Theory of Time

MS It's a matter of interdisciplinarity.

BL But doesn't this suppose another temporality, a nonmodern way of considering the passage of time?

MS This is truly the fundamental question. Whether it's the scientific hypothesis, on the one hand, which we have called the hypothesis of excellence, or, on the other hand, that of historicism, the two suppose that time develops in a linear fashion—that is, that there really is an enormous distance, more than a score of centuries, between Lucretius and today's physics. Whether this time is cumulative, continuous, or interrupted, it always remains linear.

BL Because of succession. Or successions of revolutions, as described by the epistemologists or even Foucault.

MS There you are. But time is in reality somewhat more complicated than that. You no doubt are familiar with chaos theory, which says that disorder occurring in nature can be explained, or reordered, by means of fractal attractors.

BL Yes. According to this, chance is nonetheless determined, and disorder is produced by an underlying order.

MS Exactly. But in this, order as such is harder to perceive, and customary determinism has a slightly different appearance. Time does not always flow according to a line (my first intuition of this is in my book on Leibniz [284–86]) nor according to a plan but, rather, according to an extraordinarily complex mixture, as though it reflected stopping points, ruptures, deep wells, chimneys of thunderous acceleration, rendings, gaps—all sown at random, at least in a visible disorder. Thus, the development of history truly resembles what chaos theory describes. Once you understand this, it's not hard to accept the fact that time doesn't always develop according to a line and thus things that are very close can exist in culture, but the line makes them appear very distant from one another. Or, on the other hand, that there are things that seem very close that, in fact, are very distant from one another. Lucretius and modern theory of fluids are considered as two places separated by an immense distance, whereas I see them as in the same neighborhood.

In order to explain these two perceptions we must, in fact, clarify the theory of time. The classical theory is that of the line, continuous or interrupted, while mine would be more chaotic. Time flows in an extraordinarily complex, unexpected, complicated way . . .

BL So, it is not you who travel through time but, rather, the elements that become close in this chaotic time?

MS Certainly. Time is paradoxical; it folds or twists; it is as various as the dance of flames in a brazier—here interrupted, there vertical, mobile, and unexpected.

The French language in its wisdom uses the same word for weather and time, *le temps.* At a profound level they are the same thing. Meteorological weather, predictable and unpredictable, will no doubt some day be explainable by complicated notions of fluctuations, strange attractors. . . . Someday we will perhaps understand that historical time is even more complicated.

BL In any case, it doesn't "pass."

MS Yes, it passes, and also it doesn't pass. We must bring the word *pass* closer to *passoir*—"sieve." Time doesn't flow; it percolates. This means precisely that it passes and doesn't pass. I'm very fond of the theory of percolation, which tells us things that are evident, concrete, decisive, and new about space and time.

In Latin the verb *colare,* the origin of the French verb *couler,* "to flow," means precisely "to filter." In a filter one flux passes through, while another does not.

BL But it doesn't pass in the form of a fluid. It's not a fluid.

MS Who knows?

BL It is perhaps turbulent, but not linear . . .

MS *"Sous le pont Mirabeau coule la Seine . . ."* [Beneath the Mirabeau Bridge flows the Seine . . .]—thus flows classical linear time. But Apollinaire, who had never ever navigated, at least on fresh water, hadn't studied the Seine enough. He hadn't noticed the countercurrents or the turbulences. Yes, time flows like the Seine, if one observes it well. All the water that passes beneath the Mirabeau Bridge will not necessarily flow out into the English Channel; many little trickles turn back toward Charenton or upstream.

BL They don't flow like parallel trickles.

MS It's not always laminar. The usual theory supposes time to be always and everywhere laminar. With geometrically rigid and measurable distances—at least constant. Someday it will be said that that is eternity! It is neither true nor possible. No, time flows in a turbulent and chaotic manner; it percolates. All of our difficulties with the theory of history come from the fact that we think of time in this inadequate and naive way.

BL All the theologians agree with you.

MS Really? Maybe that's why I so greatly admire Péguy's work.

BL His Clio ? *[Clio: Dialogue between History and the Pagan Soul.]*

MS Yes, *Clio.* In it one sees, from the evidence, a time that is completely turbulent.

From this you understand how Lucretius can be as close to us as our neighbor and, conversely, how contemporary things can become very distant.

BL You have a topologically bizarre space as your reference for understanding time.

MS There is in Lucretius a global theory of turbulence, which can make that time really understandable. His physics seems to me truly very advanced. Along with the contemporary sciences, it holds out the hope of a chaotic theory of time.

BL Everyone has heard you say this, and no one believes you.

MS Nonetheless, fairly simple mathematics can also easily bring one to such an idea. A certain theory of numbers reorders their sequence in such a way that near neighbors become very distant, while, inversely, distant numbers come closer. It's fun, instructive, and has a strong influence on intuition. Once you've entered into this kind of thinking you realize how much all of what we've said about time up till now abusively simplifies things.

More intuitively, this time can be schematized by a kind of crumpling, a multiple, foldable diversity. If you think about it for two minutes, this intuition is clearer than one that imposes a constant distance between moving objects, and it explains more. Everyone is amazed that after 1935 the Nazis, in the most scientifically and culturally advanced country, adopted the most archaic behavior. But we are always simultaneously making gestures that are archaic, modern, and futuristic. Earlier I took the example of a car, which can be dated from several eras; every historical era is likewise multitemporal, simultaneously drawing from the obsolete, the contemporary, and the futuristic. An object, a circumstance, is thus polychronic, multitemporal, and reveals a time that is gathered together, with multiple pleats.

BL You are explaining here a sentence I was going to ask you to explain from your book Le Tiers-Instruit, *which speaks of precisely these non-metrical diversities: "I have always used a process of abstraction like this, which could be called topological, and whose principle consists of describing non-metrical diversities—in this case, the network."*

MS Yes. If you take a handkerchief and spread it out in order to iron it, you can see in it certain fixed distances and proximities. If you sketch a circle in one area, you can mark out nearby points and measure far-off distances. Then take the same handkerchief and crumple it, by putting it in your pocket. Two distant points suddenly are close, even superimposed. If, further, you tear it in certain places, two points that were close can become very distant. This science of nearness and rifts is called topology, while the science of stable and well-defined distances is called metrical geometry.

Classical time is related to geometry, having nothing to do with space, as Bergson pointed out all too briefly, but with metrics. On the contrary, take your inspiration from topology, and perhaps you will discover the rigidity of those proximities and distances you consider arbitrary. And their sim*pli*city, in the literal sense of the word *pli* [fold]: it's simply the difference between topology (the handkerchief is folded, crumpled, shredded) and geometry (the same fabric is ironed out flat).

As we experience time—as much in our inner senses as externally in nature, as much as *le temps* of history as *le temps* of weather—it resembles this crumpled version much more than the flat, overly simplified one.

Admittedly, we need the latter for measurements, but why extrapolate from it a general theory of time? *People usually confuse time and the measurement of time,* which is a metrical reading on a straight line.

BL So mathematics, which is your model, is not metrical?

MS It can easily become so. Sketch on the handkerchief some perpendicular networks, like Cartesian coordinates, and you will define the distances. But, if you fold it, the distance from Madrid to Paris could suddenly be wiped out, while, on the other hand, the distance from Vincennes to Colombes could become infinite.

No, time does not flow as people think it does. The time we spontaneously use imitates the succession of natural integers.

BL So, it's never a case of your inventing the proximities, in your opinion? Whereas for a modernist, time passes, falls behind him, is obsolete.

MS Archaisms can always be found among us, while Lucretius, in some instances, is right on top of things, as they say.

Let me tell you a true story. Have you ever heard how some brothers, in their seventies, were grouped around their father for a funeral vigil, weeping for a dead man aged thirty or less? He had been a mountain guide and, following an accident, had disappeared into a crevasse in the high mountains. He reappeared more than a half-century later, deposited in the valley by the glacier, perfectly conserved, youthful, from the depths of the cold. His children, having grown old, prepare to bury a body that is still young. That's the source of this alpine scene, which is precisely an anachronism, and is admittedly rare here, but often observed— between a writer and his critics. Art, beauty, and profound thought preserve youth even better than a glacier!

Admire how, on the problem of time, an unpretentious true story agrees with recent science, to produce good philosophy.

BL It's precisely this biographical and philosophical bizarreness that sets you apart from modernists and makes you so difficult to read.

MS We are archaic in three-fourths of our actions. Few people and even fewer thoughts are completely congruent with the date of their times. Recall what we were saying earlier about the present.

BL Yes, but it's not enough to say it that way. A modernist could say it also. But for him it would mean that the archaic is repressed, dangerous, that it could leap out at us. Whereas for you it is a positive affirmation.

MS Why the specter of this pointless repression? Antiquity is there, most often, without needing any air pump (a truly obsolete instrument) to drive it back.

BL For you archaicism is not a holdover of which we still need to rid ourselves more completely. That would be the position of Bachelard, for example.

MS Maybe. Everything depends on the way you understand the passage of time.

Hermes, the Agent of Rapprochements

BL That's the condition, but it's not enough to clarify our reading of your texts. For example, when you tell us, as you did a little while ago, that hydrodynamics is found in Lucretius "as well," we say to ourselves, "There's another exaggeration." Because this "as well" makes us leap over great distances—distances of two thousand years, when we resurvey the time. I believe that this is the key to all the misunderstandings about your work. Those who appreciate it say, "Serres makes unexpected rapprochements that are very enlightening." Those who hate it say, "Serres again proceeds by free association." Which gives rise to the accusations of "poetry." Now we must pass from this vision of time, which is completely convincing, completely understandable, even if it is difficult . . .

MS What is hardest is not necessarily incomprehensible.

BL . . . to the second difficulty. We could understand very well a defense and an illustration of the humanities that played up the difference, saying that one must reconstruct Rome and Roman life and reimmerse Lucretius in his context. Such a historical reconstruction, which exasperated Péguy as much as it does you, doesn't pass the test—which will become your test, the Serres test: Does the past, supposedly irrational, rather than resisting historical reconstitution, find itself as solid as the newest and most contemporary rationality? But I am quite right in saying that this is by no means a question of historicism.

MS In the case of Lucretius—but perhaps this isn't the question you're asking—what functioned as a test or proof was that from the moment one poses the hypothesis of fluid mechanics, on the one hand, and the hypothesis of Archimedes, on the other, everything becomes clear, even for the keenest requirements of erudition. We hadn't noticed how much the text spoke everywhere in terms of liquidity. One would take it for Bergson, and, as far as I know, Bergson knew Lucretius very well. Even using the best criteria of the *explication de texte,* this approach works much better than the usual ones. It even allows one to correct a lot of the translation errors.

Did you ask me, "What is the condition that allows such a rapprochement?"

BL Yes, I understood clearly that the far-reaching condition is time, the crumpled time of which you spoke.

MS Folded, wadded up.

BL But then there is the question of the test. What allows you to establish the rapprochement? This is the great difficulty for your readers, who may have an impression of free association, of arbitrary rapprochements. The problem is understanding the operator that you extract. Usually, it's a form, a minimal structure that will not retain everything in Lucretius but that will extract certain elements from his work—a word, an etymology, an argument, a structure? I understand that the organization of time ensures a proximity of elements that we, as pedestrians, consider far apart. But what is the little structure, the key that allows you to link together a piece of Lucretius and a piece of physics?

MS You're asking me what I use to make the connection?

BL Yes, what tool, in essence—what hammer, what nail?

MS What tool? Here it is: today no one speaks of physics except in mathematical terms. But the physics of Lucretius is not mathematized, so it's only poetry; it can't be physics. Now at that time I was studying Archimedes' mathematics, which was considered nonsystematic. You can't detect how or why Archimedes passes through a given theorem or from the theory of spirals to that of the equilibrium of fluids. In Euclid you can see fairly clearly why: everything is systematic, based on deduction. There is no visible system in Archimedes. Now, in rereading him, I saw that the construction of his texts and his theories followed a model that was precisely that of Lucretius' physics. This is the basis for the articulation between them: on the one hand, there was the *physical model* and, on the other, the *mathematical system* that corresponded to it—what a marvel!

In other words, in antiquity physics was not mathematized as it is now. Two systems look at each other and describe the same world: one, that of Archimedes, with mathematical theorems; the other with descriptions in ordinary language, although extremely precise and exact. But both have the same object: turbulences, whirlpools, their spiral shape and their liquid nature—in short, their formation and, based on their construction, the formation of the world.

What changes is the style of the mathematization, its manner, but what endures is the mathematization itself. It consists of a correspondence of system to system and not of the processes of measurement and quantification. Once again this is very modern.

BL   This operator for bringing things closer together—you have often given it the name of Hermes. There is a primary hermeticism (in the positive sense of the word) that defines your freedom of movement. The figure of a free mediator who wanders through this folded time and who thus establishes connections . . .

MS You've named him, just as I have.

BL   But Hermes is always an arguer. Your purpose in this always is to shed light decisively on the texts, by juxtapositions that are not simply unexpected but also justified by their proximity in folded time. I understand this: it's metaphor, the standard practice of metaphor. But in my opinion there is a second hermeticism, overlying the other, contradicting it, and one that is hermetic in the sense of esoteric, intentionally abstruse, making no mediation, suppressing mediation—what I would call the Catharist aspect.

MS I don't think so. We must conceive or imagine how Hermes flies and gets about when he carries messages from the gods—or how angels travel. And for this one must describe the spaces situated between things that are already marked out—spaces of *interference,* as I called them in the title of my second book on Hermes. This god or these angels pass through folded time, making millions of connections. *Between* has always struck me as a preposition of prime importance.

Follow the flight pattern of a fly. Doesn't time sometimes flow according to the breaks and bends that this flight seems to follow or invent? Likewise, my book *Rome* describes in its own way the baker's transformation [80–84, English ed.]: a certain folding of half a plane of dough over the other half, repeated indefinitely according to a simple rule, produces a design precisely comparable to the flight of the fly or the wasp, the one Verlaine in his famous sonnet describes as drunk from his crazy flight.

BL   This passage on the flight of the fly hasn't helped to make you understood!

MS Nonetheless, it's what we call, in the most simplistic exercises, *to explicate, that is,* "to unpleat." This is an extremely complex design, incomprehensible and appearing chaotic or random, but made admirably understandable by the movements of the baker kneading his dough. He makes folds; he *implicates* something that his movements then *explicate.* The most simple and mundane gestures can produce very complicated curves.

The intermediaries—Hermes, angels, I myself as intermediary between the sciences and between science and the humanities— we are forced to fly according to these curves. Sometimes things that seem incomprehensible have causes or sources that are completely limpid, as here.

So, I can do nothing about it—time develops more like the flight of Verlaine's wasp than along a line, continuous or regularly broken by dialectical war. As a result, as soon as this intermediary comes to rest on a spot, he sometimes finds himself far off but also sometimes very close to foreignness. He always produces an effect of foreignness. The grammarian among the hydrodynamicists, the classicist among the chaos theorists, the physicist among the classicists . . . all of this seems foreign, but Lucretius, that familiar poet, brought together in himself all these characters, made diverse by our specializations.

What's more, we always believe that the expanse of the encyclopedia or of knowledge is seamless and orderly—but who said so? What if, in fact, it resembles what is produced by the baker's transformations? One of the most beautiful things that our era is teaching us is to approach with light and simplicity the very complex things previously believed to be the result of chance, of noise, of chaos, in the ancient sense of the word. Hermes the messenger first brings light to texts and signs that are hermetic, that is, obscure. A message comes through while battling against the background noise. Likewise, Hermes traverses the noise, toward meaning.

BL But the second hermeticism?

MS The second hermeticism you speak of—this effect of foreignness, this incomprehensibility—doesn't come from any paranoid solitude (I'm in good health, perfectly serene and happy, believe me), but from the ordinary effect of a messenger come from afar to announce events. The messenger always brings strange news; if not, he's nothing but a parrot. Here's the news of the day: to bring light—its clarity, of course, *but especially its speed!*—to what is most confused.

A Mathematician's Method

BL If we return to this problem of traveling from place to place, which is thus the problem of "folding" time—effecting juxtapositions—and the problem of metaphor . . .

MS Metaphor, in fact, means "transport." That's Hermes's very method: he exports and imports; thus, he traverses. He invents and can be mistaken—because of analogies, which are dangerous and even forbidden—but we know no other route to invention. The messenger's impression of foreignness comes from this contradiction: that transport is the best and the worst thing, the clearest and the most obscure, the craziest and the most certain.

BL I wanted to focus on another difficulty for readers—your argument that, once one has the principle, the rest falls into place. Once one has the structure, the rest is only consequence, conclusion, development. . . . You use this argument in a hundred different ways. You always say, "It's all in Lucretius. All of physics is already there." According to you, the structure is enough to define the situation in its entirety. Not only does this argument follow a line that's as straight as the fly's flight; what's more, this fly is in a hurry!

MS I will tell you in a minute why I'm in a hurry. An apprenticeship in philosophy takes so much work and time that one fine day one wakes up old, with no more time to consecrate to the main activity, which is getting rid of everything one knows in order to finally invent.

BL   This fly is busy and heads for structure. This is what bothers me the most in your hermetics—I who am no longer entirely a philosopher. This fly borrows only one aspect from mediate inference—rapid movement from place to place. It doesn't take anything from the other part, implying that principles don't count. What counts is precisely the system of mediate inferences, a rootedness, a localization, the slow work of intermediaries, etc. Which you don't give to us either. Of course, it's not your problem, since you want to travel rapidly. But these two difficulties—the fly's flight plus the rapidity of the fly's flight—together make reading your work very difficult.

MS Speed is the elegance of thought, which mocks stupidity, heavy and slow. Intelligence thinks and says the unexpected; it moves with the fly, with its flight. A fool is defined by predictability.

So, why this speed? My enterprise required covering everything, so I was in a hurry, since, in a brief life, to cover everything. . . . From now on you believe me, right?—since from now on the extent of my project can be read in finished books, and soon even the synthesis is coming. I have agreed to these conversations that I would have refused previously because, precisely, this view of the ensemble was not yet discernible. Yes, I have traveled everywhere—classical and modern mathematics (and mathematics is itself a world), ancient and modern physics, contemporary biology, through the so-called human sciences, when I was writing *The Parasite, Rome,* and *Statues.* Through Latin and Greek, the history of philosophy, the literature and history of religions. I have tried to speak about the essential periods—the Greeks, the Romans, the Renaissance, the seventeenth and nineteenth centuries . . . I assigned myself this undertaking as an inevitable task of preparation, and I've always been deeply hurt by accusations of being a "dabbler." Because in fact, every time I approached something it wasn't an idle voyage: I only assigned myself the undertaking on the condition that I invent something. Each time I passed somewhere I tried to leave a truly original solution. I didn't pass by Lucretius by repeating other commentators, as far as I know. Nor by Kant without discovering that he was the first to have invented an eternal return—a solution not commonplace among the specialists.

So, I traveled everywhere, and in order to do it you have to travel fast. You have to have a compendium of thought, take shortcuts.

BL Like mountain climbers who are linked together, one after another, to the one in front.

MS Yes. In such a case you need a slide to get down. You've got to go fast. But if life is brief, luckily, thought travels as fast as the speed of light. In earlier times philosophers used the metaphor of light to express the clarity of thought; I would like to use it to express not only brilliance and purity but also speed. In this sense we are inventing right now a new Age of Enlightenment.

And here is my second argument: mathematics teaches rapid thought. Whoever writes x can mean simultaneously 1, 2, 3, the infinite, rationals and transcendents, real and complex numbers, even quaternions—this is an economy of thought. When you reproach me with "Structure isn't enough; you've got to add all the intermediate steps," this is not mathematical thought. Philosophers love intermediate inferences; mathematicians gladly dispense with them. An elegant demonstration skips the intermediate steps. Indeed, there is a slowness particular to philosophers that often strikes me as affectation and a speed accompanying mathematical thought that plays with amazing shortcuts.

A lot of the incomprehension you were speaking of earlier comes simply from this speed. I am fairly glad to be living in the information age, since in it speed becomes once again a fundamental category of intelligence.

BL So, it's from math that you get your rapid movement from place to place?

MS Intuition initiates and commands, abstraction follows it, and finally proof sorts things out and sets them down, in its pedestrian way, as it can. I see myself as saying: "Notice, here, this concept sheds light on that problem. It's up to you to develop the details at your leisure. Good-bye, I've got to be going elsewhere." And, if I am mistaken, at least I won't have harmed anyone.

BL So, then, what's surprising in your method is it's mathematical aspect?

MS Yes. Springing from the need to travel quickly and evident when I show a solution.

BL And it's up to us to follow up on it.

MS Follow, follow—take up the gesture and continue it. Yes, I plead guilty and accuse myself of cutting out the intermediate steps, because the most elegant demonstration is always the shortest one.

BL This is a very important point. Your method finds its form in speed, and this speed is itself in some ways a consequence of mathematics. So, in fact, all the accusations are completely wrong; the argument about skimming and dabbling is unjustified, since, on the contrary, it's a question of being prolific.

MS Dumézil encountered the same reproaches. "Read the Vedic texts that describe funeral pyres and prayers," he said, "and consider, on the other hand, the Roman Forum and its temples, where fires burn—eternal ones in the rounded architectural forms, temporary ones in the square forms—look closely; it's the same thing." He moves quickly there, circumventing the intermediate steps, in both space and time.

Maybe there aren't any intermediate steps. Comparative methodology presupposes these leaps. Have I done anything different?

BL No, but Dumézil does it in several books.

MS True. He makes up for the speed of his demonstration by repetition, heavy and indefinite, of his thesis everywhere.

BL And there are footnotes, allowing for all the intermediate steps. Plus, he doesn't add physics!

MS Admittedly, he always remains in the same domain. But he travels rapidly in time and space. Comparativism proceeds by short circuits and, as we see in electricity, this produces dazzling sparks.

BL Dumézil brings things together within a domain but justified fanatically and meticulously through intermediate steps.

MS Yes.

BL While you, you are fanatical about skipping over the intermediate steps!

MS In the field of comparativism, since we are talking about it, the threads to be dealt with or woven together are more tangled;

they go farther or have a farther influence, in both time and space and among disciplines. The space *between*—that of conjunctions, the interdisciplinary ground—is still very much unexplored. One must travel quickly when the thing to be thought about is complex.

Have you noticed the popularity among scientists of the word *interface*—which supposes that the junction between two sciences or two concepts is perfectly under control, or seamless, and poses no problems? On the contrary, I believe that these spaces *between* are more complicated than one thinks. This is why I have compared them to the Northwest Passage [in *Hermès V. Le Passage du Nord-Ouest*], with shores, islands, and fractal ice floes. Between the hard sciences and the so-called human sciences the passage resembles a jagged shore, sprinkled with ice, and variable. Have you seen the map of northern Canada? Once again the path of this passage strangely resembles what I earlier called the fly's flight pattern. It's more fractal than truly simple. Less a juncture under control than an adventure to be had. This is an area strangely void of explorers.

Style, or Mathematics Continued by Other Means

BL Things are slowly becoming clearer to me. You have imported into philosophy a mathematical style of argumentation. In your opinion this is your greatest contribution. The metalanguage that you have chosen (I realize that the word metalanguage isn't right) is philosophical argumentation. You are very much a technical philosopher in the long tradition of argumentation, but your style of demonstration is borrowed from mathematics.

MS It is algebraic or topological, issuing from structural mathematics, born in this century.

And what we learn from this famous revolution that separates classical and modern mathematics—the most dazzling thing about it—is precisely the ensemble of leaps we were just talking about. We can compare an ordinary algebraic theorem and one from distant geometry or from arithmetic. Suddenly, two or three objects separated by great distances, with no previous link between them, belong to the same family. This way of thinking or of operating makes whoever uses it an authentic structuralist, even if the word has lost both its original sense and its importance in methodology.

BL This is the technical basis of your comparativism.

MS That's it, or, rather, I began with it. I had learned it in contemporary algebra and in topology. Which is the source of the difficulties you speak of—this elimination of intermediate inferences.

The advantage that results from it is a new organization of knowledge; the whole landscape is changed. In philosophy, in which elements are even more distanced from one another, this method at first appears strange, for it brings together the most disparate things. People quickly criticized me for this—for bringing together turbulence theory and Lucretius' poetry, thermodynamics and Zola's novels, and so on. But these critics and I no longer have the same landscape in view, the same overview of proximities and distances. With each profound transformation of knowledge come these upheavals in perception.

BL Nonetheless, when you behave like a rigorous comparativist, the kindest thing they say about you is, "It's not rigorous, but it's well written." Now, if I understand rightly, for you style is always . . .

MS Rapidity. To move, while writing, from one point of the universe to another.

BL Yes, but there isn't a formal mathematical language that allows you to do this, is there?

MS Not always, obviously.

BL So, you are obliged, for philosophical reasons, to move from mathematics to style?

MS I'm delighted you mentioned that! For this reason I was irrevocably condemned to abandon the classical or technical style of philosophy, because, as far as I could see, it didn't have the terms or operators capable of describing this method.

BL Is it because these terms aren't precise enough, aren't rapid enough?

MS No doubt. I was condemned to invent a new vocabulary, which would have complicated the situation even more, so little by little

I resolved to use more and more natural, everyday language. But the moment you refine language as much and as well as possible, you create a style.

This is the reason for that "poetic" effect—a strange accusation that I have suffered from and still do—not because I scorn poetry but because this is evidence of solid incomprehension. For a new situation it was necessary to find a new language. As I've said before, classically and repetitively, technical language disgusts me—I've already explained why.

BL But the superego that watches over the selection of this style is still the succession of argumentations we've just reviewed. Philosophy possesses the metalanguage; it is tormented by an urgency to move from place to place. This philosophy has structural mathematics as its means or matrix . . .

MS Comparativism and the complexity of things and of time require swift movement and a new style.

BL It's incredible the way you have accumulated misunderstandings!

MS Nonetheless, I have always written as clearly and distinctly as possible.

BL Every element in your method has been misunderstood. It's assumed that you go your own way in order to avoid methodological constraints altogether, that you distance yourself as much as possible from mathematics, and that, if you arrive at style, it's for literary reasons, and not at all for technical reasons. Now, if I've understood rightly, style, in fact, is best if it imitates mathematics as precisely as possible, in a domain mathematics can't enter.

MS At least the rigor and precision of mathematics. Does Plato himself proceed otherwise? Every time he has something somewhat difficult to say, he abandons technical vocabulary and goes to myth, telling a story that globalizes his point even more. He is always in the process of moving obliquely, as you said. Where neither mathematics nor logic can go, let myth go! Which is the reason, in Plato and in so many others, for the asides, the leaps, the ruptures, the demonstrations in the narrative, from metaphysics to folktales. Leibniz, in his *Theodicy*, proceeds in no other way. There's nothing so extraordinary in this.

BL But these are allegories, which follow rules.

MS Mine follow rules, too.

Literature under Surveillance by Philosophy

BL That's precisely it—you don't leave the rational will of philosophical demonstration, any more than Plato does. For you, too, the classical virtue of philosophy continues to be the synthesis.

MS Yes, I'm racing toward a synthesis. No doubt it will be unexpected in relation to the totals and subtotals that can be arrived at now. Why? Because this synthesis will no doubt be made more through comparativism than by sequential linking, more through Hermes's swift travels than by deduction or solid construction. In fact, Hermes transports forms from one place to another via fluxes in the air. The synthesis will be made, more probably, among fluids.

BL So, now I understand what you are saying in Le Tiers-Instruit: *"Where mathematics can't go, let myth go, and where myth does not want to go, let Gascon dialect go."*

MS "Where the French language can't go, let Gascon go." It's a quote from Montaigne's *Essays.* Should we footnote it?

BL It's also constantly in contradiction, in tension with the fact that the point of departure and the trajectory are under strict philosophical surveillance. This is a difficulty for your readers. One could say, "All right, knowing that philosophy's technical language can't go there, let literature go." But not a single page of yours is literature; each page is constantly—I won't say on a leash—but under philosophical surveillance. Now, then, your argument is different. Philosophy, being under philosophical surveillance, knows why literature has always kept its distance. It's a good paradox.

MS Yes and no. But it would be nice to write real literature, either without surveillance, or, rather, with another type of surveillance. I dream about it, but I probably can't do it.

BL Rather, if I've understood rightly, you don't want to do it.

MS No doubt, I neither know how nor can. Rousseau is an excellent example. I admire unreservedly the supreme gracefulness with which he glides easily from *La Nouvelle Héloïse*—one of the most beautiful novels and no doubt the most well written in our language—to *The Social Contract.* Once again, in the French-language tradition, Montaigne, Pascal, Diderot, and Voltaire make this transition easily.

Why? Because besides creating concepts, philosophy creates characters. It was Deleuze again who recently said it best, in a way that I can't. Here are some of these characters: Hermes, the Parasite, the Hermaphrodite, Harlequin, and "Le Tiers-Instruit"—"the Instructed Third, knowledge's troubadour." But how can we let them be free to live and to come and go? The sciences themselves know of those angels whom you yourself have elsewhere called "delegates," or envoys, sent to observe more subtly than we can.

The obstacle comes from divisions, both ancient and very recent, imposed by academia. The passage is natural, and the obstacle is artificial. Basically, you are interrogating me about an artifact.

BL No, you could write literature, but you don't want to, since your style is one of philosophical argument continued by other means, imitating mathematical work . . .

MS Imitating or, better, transposing, exporting, translating the work of mathematicians.

BL To a place where mathematics cannot go.

MS All the difficulties, all the obstacles, all the conditions for these transportings, transferals, and translations, including the Parasite (as human character, animal, and noise), including the lighthouses (which make passages possible and which maritime logs call "lights and fog horns" [*Feux et signaux de brume*]) are laid out in detail in my books. These books meditate on successful communication, as in Leibniz or Hermes, or, on the contrary, on the interceptions that make communication difficult or impossible. For example, *Genesis* (which should have been called *Noise,* an old French word that expresses clamor and furor) speaks of background noise, just as the Parasite links this background noise to an operator—either physical, animal, or human. Hermes's great enterprise continues.

One of my upcoming books will be devoted to angels—kinds of messengers who take a thousand forms. They describe and travel throughout a world closely resembling our own.

But communication also involves methodological transfers from one science to another, or from the purest science to philosophy. Communication traverses those spaces—for example, that of the encyclopedia—that are much less clear and transparent than one would have believed. If you review the titles of my books, you will be able to retrace easily how I passed from mathematics to physics, from physics to the life sciences and to the human sciences, without ever leaving behind their historical component. But these don't make up a seamless list or category, occupying a homogeneous or flat space; on the contrary, they suggest a tormented, hilly landscape—chaotic, fractal, more faithful to reality.

Indeed, the classification of the sciences has changed a lot in thirty years; one hesitates to classify at all. No doubt, the information age will someday bring us an en*cliqu*opedia!

BL This way of presenting the argument changes everything. It's not a rupture with philosophy. Or, rather, it's a huge rupture from the point of view of the field, extension and construction of time—but it is inserted in a traditional project.

MS Yes, it doesn't differ from philosophy's traditional project. I never plead originality—rather, in fact, classicism.

BL But, if you were writing literature, your readers would never suspect that literature goes farther than philosophy! The surveillance of argumentation in your texts is not diminished; rather, it is increased.

MS How could I abandon that kind of surveillance? This alertness conditions rational work.

BL At the same time, your philosophical project does not aim to cloak the text in your metalanguage but, instead, to use the metalanguage of writers, of myths—so that it does your philosophical or scientific work for you. You certainly don't make things easy for us!

MS But are things themselves easy?

Basically, when you have no available model, when you're wandering in the desert, you don't always see things clearly. The constant presence of a scientific community, of ongoing debate, peer pressure—things we talked about earlier, so lacking for me—all these contribute powerfully to clarifying what you say. Solitude often accompanies difficulty, explains it. When two people are together, as we are today, debate already begins to clarify things. So, you see, I'm beginning to evolve, on the question of discussion.

Demonstration and Interpretation

Bruno Latour: Last time, you will recall, we spoke about your methodology. I had tried to make a list of the misunderstandings surrounding your work.

Michel Serres: Yes, I recall its great length.

BL Fairly long, indeed. But we had clarified three points that for me were decisive: that of your style, that of mathematical formalism, and that of time, of your conception of time. These three hang together. Your style allows you to continue to use formalism in areas that heretofore had not lent themselves to it, in what could be called generalized comparativism. This comparativism itself is completely linked to the fact that you do not believe in linear time. Consequently, these delicate interpretations that you compared to a fly's flight pattern and that your readers take as nonchalance . . .

MS As arbitrariness.

BL . . . in fact, correspond to an extremely precise way of moving about in subjects for which the usual formalism has no concepts.

MS Because of the folded or crumpled time we talked about.

BL My questions today will focus on formal proof, on demonstration—on what enables you to decide whether an interpretation you offer is right or not.

The Ins and Outs of Interpretation

BL I'd like to talk about the second hermeticism, which is in a sense darker, less positive, than the first one. In our difficulties in reading you, I'd like to understand what is philosophically necessary and what is contingent—due to particular circumstances. For the former, we have said enough about it—it's up to the reader to work it out—but for the latter...

MS It's up to the author?

BL Yes, it's up to the author! I didn't dare say it.

MS All right, let's get to work. I've never proposed an interpretation nor posed a question without there first being a problem. Let's choose an example other than Lucretius: Verlaine's sonnet that begins, "Hope shines like a wisp of hay in the stable, what do you fear from the wasp, drunk from his crazy flight?" This text, which is really incomprehensible, always remains an enigma, after thousands of attempts at interpretation. Luckily, we spoke earlier about the flight pattern of flies and obstacles to communication; this will help us here.

In the sonnet Verlaine describes someone who falls asleep, his elbow on the table, in the summer noontime heat, while hearing the hum of a wasp's flight. This is an ordinary coenesthetic experience: perceived by the body itself, or internally, in which the wandering sound, the noise perceived, comes both from the external world and from the organism itself. Now, in saying this, the poet comes close to contemporary theories on background noise.

BL Contemporary to Verlaine or to us?

MS To us, although he's separated from us by a century. By observing his own intropathic experience with what I dare to call an unheard-of precision, Verlaine intuits the reality of background noise, which precedes all signals and is an obstacle to their perception—anterior to any language and either hindering or assisting its arrival. Inversely, the intense sound of language prevents us from hearing this sound.

As a result, the observer provides a sort of genesis of language, or of everything that takes place before its appearance. Now here's a subject that's truly poetic; at the same time it's a real, scientific object. The time lapse between these two propositions measures the historical distance between Verlaine and us.

If you accept such a hypothesis, the enigma is resolved, and the sonnet becomes clear and transparent. The moment you bring transparency and clarity to a problem, the interpretation is probably a good one; what was inexplicable becomes illuminated.

BL The interpretation is good, but it seems implausible.

MS It only seems implausible to those who believe that an unbridgeable distance separates a nineteenth-century poet from a late-twentieth-century physicist. Why shouldn't an experience that at the time remained in the domain of introspection, reserved for those focusing subtly on an object not usually observed—why shouldn't it later become a collective, physical object of study? It would not be the first time that such a thing happens.

BL Wait a minute—there are two difficulties, two improbabilities. We talked before in detail about the first one: that Verlaine could anticipate the results of the physics of noise, which come a century later.

MS Yes.

BL Your conception of time makes this possible. This is why I spoke last time about a machine for traveling backward in time; in fact, it's not the right expression . . .

MS It's not a "machine for traveling backward in time," because in that phrase the words *machine* and *backward in time* bother me. Set in motion on its railroad track, such a locomotive is the perfect embodiment of linear time, even if it is traveling backward!

BL Then I'll withdraw my expression. I was trying to express your freedom of movement. All right, there is neither machine nor rail nor traveling backward. But at the same time, and this is the second difficulty, you don't actually say that Verlaine anticipates physics, since you are careful to maintain a distance between the poem and Brillouin's book on noise.

MS But, yes, I will say willingly that he anticipates—why not? The great poets, the philosophers themselves, often anticipate. What good is philosophy if it doesn't give birth to the world of the future?

Do you suffer from acoustic phenomena, from that constant whistling in the ears, which never ceases, day or night? If so, you will concede that the perceptual experience of background noise is not so rare. A poet is generally sensitive to his own coenesthesia and is subtly aware of the internal and secret rapport within the body itself. The noise I'm talking about—springing from the organism, constantly testifying to its intense heat, to its life, perhaps announcing its death—can only be stilled by music, can only be forgotten through language. This aspect of finality in language and singing is rarely expressed. Verlaine's sonnet describes with genius this anteriority of noise to music and poetic language as well as the obstacle it presents to these two currents of signals.

Do you think that a theoretician of poetry or music can ignore such preexisting conditions? One can reasonably think that Verlaine is giving here an anticipatory intuition of what will become, for us, the theory of background noise as it relates to language messages.

Is there a big difference between the theoretical expression of the message, defending itself physically against the background noise, and the grasp of language that a poet can have in relation to the noise he hears in his own coenesthesis? Is the similarity so amazing? Great scientific intuitions sometimes have a Spartan-like simplicity. It's said that Wegener had the idea of the theory of plate tectonics while watching the spring breakup of the ice floes. Every traveler, every Eskimo has seen this common event. Apples fall for everyone, but a little differently under Newton's gaze.

BL You're going too fast!—because there are a lot of problems in what you say, which are precisely those had in general by your readers. First you say, "There have been thirty interpretations of Verlaine." In this you need to acknowledge that your demonstration continues a body of discussion by colleagues and other learned people, whom you never mention in your books.

MS If one had to recopy everything one had read, books would become alarmingly obese. Even more important, this repetition would make them not very informative. The day that every text copies or summarizes that part of the library that concerns it, we will enter the age of the thesis, of the newspaper, and of stuttering. Much as they detest each other, the press and academia have this repetitiveness in common. Theses and popular magazines—the same duplication.

On the other hand, honesty consists of writing only what one thinks and what one believes oneself to have invented. My books come only from me. "My glass is not big, but I drink from it." That's my only quote. Don't you laugh at learned articles in which each word is flanked by a number, whose corresponding footnote attributes that word to an owner, as though proper names were soon going to replace common nouns? Common nouns belong to everyone, and in an honest book the ideas come from the author.

One word on that word *author*, which comes to us from Roman law and means "the guarantor of authenticity, of loyalty, of an affirmation, of a testimony or an oath," but primitively it means "he who augments"—not he who borrows, summarizes, or condenses, but only he who makes grow. *Author, augmenter...* everything else is a cheat. A work evolves by growing, like a tree or an animal.

BL I'm familiar with your opinion on footnotes, but your reader never hears your argumentation about why your predecessors' ideas are unsatisfactory.

MS The reader arrives newborn before the text.

BL Not only does he arrive newborn—without your quoting from those you are opposing—what's more, in your books the reader usually doesn't arrive before the text, which is not even quoted, but before your idiosyncratic commentary, which is doubly allusive! In the case of Verlaine we're lucky: the entire sonnet is quoted. But, usually, you must admit, we have neither the text nor the interpretations of those who, according to you, are mistaken about the text.

MS You seem to think that no idea exists or blooms except in opposition to another or others. This harks back to our previous discussion on debate. An idea opposed to another idea is always the same idea, albeit affected by the negative sign. The more you oppose one another, the more you remain in the same framework of thought.

New ideas come from the desert, from hermits, from solitary beings, from those who live in retreat and are not plunged into the sound and fury of repetitive discussion. The latter always makes too much noise to enable one to think easily. All the money that is scandalously wasted nowadays on colloquia should be spent on building retreat houses, with vows of reserve and silence. We have more than enough debates; what we need are some taciturn people. Perhaps science needs ongoing public discussions; philosophy would surely perish from them.

BL But you need to understand our problems, as readers. Not only are there no footnotes, not only do you not reproduce the text you're talking about, which we are supposed to know (and we need to know a lot when we read you—Lucretius, Latin, Greek, physics, mathematics, poetry), but, on top of all this, in the interest of simplification, we must accept an invisible operator, a shortcut that allows you to say, "There you are; this demonstration is accurate, enlightening, satisfying." You must admit that you don't make the job easy for us!

Necessary Difficulties and Contingent Difficulties

MS I'm quite willing to shed light on these difficulties.

BL I'm sure that you can!

MS Let's take another example. I once tried to explain Pascal's *Pensées* based on his scientific works, or, more accurately, to explain the two works at the same time—his writings on mathematics or physics and the *Pensées,* based on their common intuition, that of the fixed point. In fact, this intuition gives a unity that belongs to theorems and algorithms, a unity that carries over to philosophical meditations.

On the one hand, Pascal's studies on the stasis, balance, or equilibrium of liquids show the search for a fixed point that makes balance possible. But there are also his studies of conical sections and the magic squares, or the famous arithmetical triangle. We see here a nice continuum in the scientific thought of the author, whose sparse articles reflect only the spin-off from one thought. Now, this same fixed point can be found in his "reason of effects," in the two infinities, and especially in all his meditations on Jesus Christ, considered as the center toward which everything gravitates.

The rapprochement of scientific discovery and religious conversion is drastically and mutually illuminating. So, it could be said that for Pascal it is not so much a question of *Les Pensées* but, rather, of a *single* thought at work in all his writings, without distinction of genre. To discover thus the unity, where tradition saw only dispersion, is illuminating, wouldn't you say? Further, not so long ago a professor of literature could explain this author based on Latin, on the theological or ritualistic tradition of the Catholic Church. Why? Because there was a cultural community linking Pascal or the seventeenth century to students of the time, which allowed for an explanation springing from that base. But this community has disappeared, at least temporarily, and today's students are much more familiar with arithmetic, with Newton's binomial, with triangles and probability theory than with the theological debate over the divine nature of Jesus Christ. One age has been torn apart; another has been sewn together. So, henceforth it is to the advantage of a professor of literature to explain Pascal as I do, rather than in the old-fashioned way.

Here again it could be said that time has been crumpled in a different way. The old divisions collapse, so that what formerly was incomprehensible becomes evidence itself and, conversely, what seemed self-evident presents immense difficulties. Latin has become as rare as Sanskrit was in my day, and science, which you used to find so difficult, has become commonplace in everyday life and in the press. Consequently, explaining Verlaine's poem in the light of communication theory, background noise, and the quasi-physical origin of language is going to become as simple as saying hello.

The evidence that I'm seeking to produce is thus double: it concerns the content of the demonstration—something simple (a fixed point, what could be more simple?) is always easier to grasp than scattered diversity. On the other hand, this evidence is addressed to people—contemporaries—whose culture has just remodeled itself as perhaps never before. There's objective conviction about the subject itself, subjective (or rather collective) conviction in relation to interlocutors.

BL I agree, that seems convincing. But that's what I was trying to say a little while ago: there are certain difficulties inherent in your method— we've talked about that—and then difficulties that I would call contingent, circumstantial. As soon as you position your interpretations in opposition to a group of colleagues, and in support of others who take them up, use them, or discuss them, everything becomes completely understandable. In philosophy this is "business as usual." You simply insert yourself in a scientific field. But at the same time you conceal this opposition and this support from us. And in their place, if I may say so, you add difficulties. You stress the unique, radically new, untrammeled character of your arguments, having neither antecedents nor derivatives.

MS You keep imagining that science and philosophy are the same business, as you might say in today's jargon. I will perhaps concede science to you, which admittedly remains a collective practice, but I am sure that philosophy is not the same business, and even that it is not a business at all. In any case, it differs greatly from what you call the scientific field.

For the rest, if I described earlier the solitude of my research, its isolation, I never claim that it is exceptional. I have also stressed the completely classical philosophical tradition to which I attach myself. The relationship between the sciences and philosophy, the relationship of literature to these—this is the daily bread of all philosophers throughout the history that is theirs. In this we are never alone; in fact we live in very good company!

BL Yes. It's possible, given your formation, which we talked about in our first conversation. But what seems very important to me is that these "contingent difficulties" are not linked to your philosophy. This is contrary to other possible readings of your works. Some people say, "Serres is difficult to read, and this difficulty is completely linked to the philosophical argument itself." But, if I understand rightly, this link is, in fact, not so complete.

MS I would like to believe that, in fact, the latter argument is simply related to an effect of history and situation—the one we lived through in 1950, at a particular moment, in a restricted space.

BL There is no reason in the argument itself to have to add "neither master nor disciple." It's an important point; it's not necessary.

MS I have a great repugnance for master-disciple relationships. "Here, I am your servant": this declaration would give me a lasting disgust for the master's power.

We work as philosophers. If we were practicing a science, we would necessarily have to belong to a structured discipline—structured in its content as well as its institutions—whence the organized game of teaching, of masters and pupils, of research labs and patrons, of journals and publications. The choice of philosophy supposes an altogether different behavior—independence, freedom of thought, escape from lobbying support groups . . . and therefore, indeed, solitude. I repeat: this is not a question of being exceptional but, rather, of being independent. Highly organized groups stress monitoring; it is no doubt desirable in the sciences and leads to rigorousness, if not to conformity. In philosophy this would be like police surveillance. Contrary to what Plato said, give philosophers everything you wish, except power—even intellectual, local, and partial power.

BL Yes, but that's a whole different problem. Your argumentation doesn't resemble a position like Nietzsche's, in favor of aphorism over the philosophical style. You don't want to abolish demonstration. So, for you it is always a matter of argumentation, of proof. You aren't irrational. But it so happens that, given the intellectual resources of the predominant disciplines, your proofs don't "play." But in an academic environment, in which you would have had four or five people like Dumézil and three or four like René Girard . . .

MS If intellectual formation were bipolar, letters-sciences, the thing would have been not only playable but already played! Instead of having to create a discipline, it would have already existed. In which case I might have done something else. You can't redo either history or your own life.

BL This is an important point for your readers.

MS Do you think so? I have tried to forge links where there were nothing but schisms, and this attempt was made at a very high price—that of not being understood, since there was no common language bridging this schism. In a dialogue you hear a speaker but never the interpreter. I took on this game, knowing that I would have to pay dearly for its conditions and obligations. To be without master or disciple, as you describe it, assuredly comes from an ethical decision, but it also comes from historical circumstances.

Synthesis Is Finally Possible

BL So, do I understand that for you a global will to explain does exist?

MS Of course! The other day, apropos of crumpled or folded time, we talked about the present and the past, but not about the future. Now, philosophy is an anticipation of future thoughts and practices. If not, it would be reduced to commentary—to a subcategory of history, and not the best one either. Or else to a subcategory of linguistics or logic, and not the best of these either. Not only must philosophy invent, but it invents the common ground for future inventions. *Its function is to invent the conditions of invention.* This is true for Aristotle, Descartes, Leibniz . . . all the way up to Bergson.

BL Including scientific invention?

MS Assuredly. It's necessary to talk about the future of science, which, since the Age of Enlightenment, and ever more forcefully, recruits the best intellects, the most efficient technical and financial means. As a result, science finds itself in a dominant position, at the top of the heap, as we say, single-handedly preparing the future and in a position to occupy more and more territory. Powerful and isolated, it runs—or could run and make others run— grave risks. Why? Because it knows nothing about culture. As Aesop said about language, science has become by far the best and perhaps the worst of things.

BL So, now perhaps it's science that we must save, that we must defend? Hope still remains in Pandora's box, but we must go down into the black box to seek it.

MS That's it. As soon as inventions or scientific results and projects pose redoubtable global questions, touching people's lives or the survival of the globe, we hear the cry, "Let's form ethics committees; let's bring in the legal profession, philosophers, the clergy." Then they summon the few who are still around . . . to meetings and to discuss . . .

Formerly, my work consisted of preparing for the moment when we would pay the true price of the consequences of science's takeover of all reason, culture, and morality. We are at that moment. We are paying for the illusion of progress, especially for the illusion of having no archaisms in our baggage. Alas, no—archaism is always there, and science doesn't get rid of it. Henceforth we are in danger because culture, whose job it was to slowly direct these archaisms, risks being destroyed by a science stripped of this function. My work consisted of foreseeing this moment.

Our generation had an inkling of this day of reckoning, since it saw the dawn of the atomic bomb. Hiroshima was truly the end of one world and the beginning of a new adventure. Science had just gained such power that it could virtually destroy the planet. That makes a big impression. Science's rise to power supposes such a level of recruitment that soon, all-powerful, it creates a vacuum around itself. Which is the reason for the sudden decline of all the surrounding areas of culture—the humanities, arts, religion, even the legal system.

Science has all the power, all the knowledge, all the rationality, all the rights, too, of course, all plausibility or legitimacy, admittedly—but at the same time all the problems and soon all the responsibilities. So, all of a sudden we have a time that is curiously folded, since suddenly everything is tied together in one particular spot.

BL So, the future has the same topological configuration as the past, which we talked about before, and which you were referring to a few minutes ago?

MS Of course. But the future still remains unpredictable. Fortunately!

BL For you the past is also unpredictable, if I understand correctly?

MS Yes and no.

BL This is important for us, your readers, because in your books you play both repertoires, especially in your two most recent books. In these two books, The Natural Contract *and* Le Tiers-Instruit, *you stress the second hermetic practice: the necessity for total solitude, for freedom from all bonds. Now, if I have understood rightly what you are saying, all these problems of rapprochement, of moving around, of agenda and of mobilization—of intellectual strategy—are not philosophically linked to solitude; they are contingently linked to solitude.*

MS One can work, think, and discover without any strategy at all. Believe me, none of my books is the result of a tactic.

More generally, a single answer to all questions seems improbable; a single key will not open all locks. Why would you want invention to follow a single track, always collective and dialectical? If this were true, it would be known; everyone would invent. Perhaps one is made to believe it in order to nourish the illusion that everyone invents?

There are connections and ruptures; there are the solidary and the solitary and surely others besides, who take flight and alight at crossroads.

BL Have you always had this will toward synthesis?

MS Yes, please believe me, in all earnestness. It was there from the beginning, in what a while ago I called my project. I was hoping for a philosophy for these questions—so new—when I resigned from the Naval Academy, three years after Hiroshima. Our generation heard in that event an extraordinary call from the contemporary era to think about a problem that had never been posed in the past, which could not be found in books. Faced with this global "take-off" and these global dangers, we need a global philosophy.

BL I don't understand this take-off—is it so new, so unheard of?

MS Yes, totally new.

The last chapter of *The Natural Contract* consists of a global account, in which several short tales are brought together, all tending toward a single and unique lesson: a study of the concrete root of the word *contract*—the connection, the cord, attached or detached. *Contract* means that some collectivity is working together to *pull*, or draw, something—a plow, a burden. In order to do so, there must be ties that link the pullers, or "tractors," to one another and to the thing pulled. This is the source of my continued meditation on cords—the visible ones that link the ship to the quay as well as those that make the boat a giant latticework of knots, those that bind mountain climbers together or woodcutters to the fallen tree they haul in unison (as described in *The Natural Contract*). Then there are those invisible ties that join together lovers and families, the living to life or to death, and mankind to the Earth. And, suddenly, we cast off all these ties; we untie them; humanity takes off. From where? How? Toward what? These are our questions today. But it is only through the powers of science that we have taken off like this.

BL Yes, but this will toward synthesis, which is surely in your written work, is at the same time completely concealed. I have the impression that this is the first time you have spoken of it.

MS Indeed, I am expressing it for the first time—I actually agreed to these conversations in order to express it publicly. But that does not mean that I didn't have the hope of it before me for a long time now. Chaos only appears to be chaos because one does not yet have a good theory of chaos. My work is at the point just before everything gels. In three minutes it will gel.

BL That presupposes people who will stay with it, take it up, debate it.

MS What does it matter? We will see.

BL Nothing in what you say seems unrealistic or even shocking. On the contrary, what shocks me more is the impression, perhaps false, that some of the difficulties of reading your work are added, that you have inserted them, in some sort. This elegant work of argumentation and proof is constantly hidden behind a barrage of refutation aimed at colleagues who march to a different drummer and behind supporting discussions. What I'm saying is, is your goal still that of philosophy?

MS Absolutely. I never intended to engage in anything except philosophy, in its historical tradition. And, if I produce some effect of foreignness, this astonishes me.

BL You wouldn't be exaggerating a bit there?

MS No, truly. At finding myself in the oldest tradition of Montaigne or Diderot?

BL In reading Le Tiers-Instruit, *one can't tell if the difficulties I spoke of are essential or contingent.*

MS No doubt the greatest difficulty lies in my wish to be encyclopedic, followed by my desire for synthesis, in the hope of going everywhere, of not missing anything, in order to gradually build a world. None of that was fashionable, formerly. The era of suspicion and of hypercriticism only spoke of fragments, of local pieces, of criticizing and destroying. So, it was necessary to leap aside to avoid being dragged along. Assembling, accumulating facts, the voyage into the totality of knowledge and experiences—these admittedly have their difficulties, depending on the content, but they also presuppose a distancing on the part of the person doing it.

BL So, it's not so easy to distinguish between these two hermetic practices?

MS There's only one, strictly speaking. Hermes is a complex god but unique among his kind.

On the other hand, don't you think the philosopher is pulled between two poles—that of maximal accumulation of all knowledge and experience and, at the other extreme, the cancellation of all knowledge and experience, starting from zero? Philosophy works on a two-layered cone, occupying its apex. I see the encyclopedia on the first layer and, on the second, nothing—learned unknowing, the suspension of judgment, solitude, questioning, doubt, incertitude, reconstruction starting from zero. Philosophy is not a body of knowledge nor a discipline among the usual sciences, because it insists on this balance between everything and nothing. A philosophical work necessarily contains everything, and then everything starting from nothing, through a newness obtained by this leap aside. Thus, the difficulty is double and redoubtable: it concerns the accumulation of the totality and the foreignness of the leap aside.

The Proper Use of Commentary

BL It's a question that we'll leave open. For me there are two hermetic practices—one that multiplies the mediate inferences, the other that annuls them—and I see in your recent works an exacerbation of this conflict, but you yourself are not quite sure about it. In both cases an interpretation is judged, in the best philosophical tradition, by its degree of coherence, by its alignment with a synthesis that you yourself are seeking.

MS On the first layer of the cone, mediate inferences perhaps multiply. But on the second they are annulled. Be that as it may, the synthesis I'm talking about is on its way.

BL But here we arrive at a new problem for the reader. One of the most amazing effects in your work, and one of the most difficult to understand, is the fact that the metalanguage comes always from the thing in question and not from the methodology used. It's a metalanguage imprisoned, crystallized or frozen within the very texts you use to make your explication.

This makes it very difficult for a reader to know whether or not a demonstration is convincing.

MS Two things: I avoid metalanguage, because usually it is only used for publicity. What's the point of saying, "I just did this or that"? If one really does it, it's obvious.

But, even more important, a single key won't open all locks, as I just said. (At least there's only one that does—the passkey.) Philosophy doesn't consist of marshaling ready-made solutions proffered by a particular method or parading all those problems in a category resolved by this method. Because there is no universal method.

Which is the reason, to answer your question, for drawing an appropriate method from the very problem one has undertaken to resolve. Thus, the best solutions are local, singular, specific, adapted, original, regional. This is the source of the disparity you were complaining about, which makes for difficult reading. Obviously, the work is not streamlined—not for the reader, and especially not for the author, because each time he tackles a problem he has to start over again at zero. Everyone enjoys the familiar—always reading the same books, seeing the same paintings, eating the same cake every Sunday. Don't confuse conviction and indolence! Universal metalanguage is comfortable and lazy.

Conversely, the best synthesis only takes place on a field of maximal differences—striped like a zebra or a tiger, knotted, mixed together—a harlequin's cape. If not, the synthesis is merely the repetition of a slogan.

What do you think of those painters who are instantly recognized because they always paint the same picture? They are churning out counterfeit banknotes, easily recognizable.

BL *We're touching on a more general problem, since until your last five books you, in fact, wrote commentaries on texts, and at the same time you often could not find words harsh enough to denounce commentators. In what way are your commentaries different from those of others?*

MS The commentaries I used to criticize could be called imperialistic. (I don't do it anymore; it's indifferent to me now, because commentary itself is too parasitic on invention.) They were imperialistic because they used a single key to open all doors and windows; they used a passkey that was psychoanalytical or Marxist or semiotic, and so on. Obviously, imperialism concerns not only content or method but also the institution: this or that academic department or campus follows this or that school, at the exclusion of all others. Academia is not a place in which freedom of thought really flourishes.

To me, however, singularities were important, local detail for which a simplistic passkey was not sufficient. On the contrary, what was necessary was a tool adapted to the problem. No work without this tool. You have to invent a localized method for a localized problem. Each time you try to open a different lock, you have to forge a specific key, which is obviously unrecognizable and without equivalent in the marketplace of method. Your baggage quickly becomes quite heavy. On the other hand, what you call metalanguage is easily recognizable—the repetition of the same key, available everywhere, widespread, and supported by a publicity campaign.

BL I can easily understand this need to retool, to recast the tools of analysis each time one tackles a new object.

MS Every time. This is why a localized vocabulary is necessary, to get as close as possible to the beast in question. How can you talk about carpentry without knowing its vocabulary, about nautical matters without its own lexicon, about blacksmithing without that of the forge, about cobbling without that of awl and leather, and so on? This concerns style as well as methodology or demonstration. Formerly, one learned in school to use the proper word and never to write *flower* or *herb tea,* which are too abstract and general, but to specify *gentian* or *linden tea.* A professional writer always uses a lot of different words, since he prefers *open-beam ceiling* to *cathedral ceiling,* which doesn't exist in farmhouses, and *dory* or *skiff* to *boat,* which is rarely usable for this or that fishing expedition in heavy seas. The average reader may complain that he has to look things up in the dictionary, but the sailor and the carpenter will rejoice that they are respected. In his old age Victor Hugo spoke of "revolutionizing" the old dictionary; this means, in fact, no longer using the general word *rope* but using in each case the specific term used by the specialist. As a result, the entire population, blacksmith and cobbler, hears his language spoken.

BL And does metalanguage seem parasitic in philosophy as well?

MS Not always, but often. I am appalled by those texts in which each word, each concept, or every operation is overshadowed by the substantive or the verb *to be,* to the point where the page, smooth and homogeneous, is like a desert. Sterile, facile. There is nothing new under such a sun. In just such a way the atomic bomb vitrifies the plain over which it explodes. There is nothing but that sun, there is nothing but that bomb; everything exists, nothing exists. Much more livable, wouldn't you agree, is a countryside of gently rolling hills, diverse and multiple, agreeable and varied—in other words, pluralism?

Whether or not he's a philosopher, whoever writes is like an organist; he must change registers and pull out in turn the various stops: the *bourdon,* the *nasard,* the cornet, the canon, the krummhorn, or the *larigot.* There—you are going to criticize me for adding to the difficulties and differences of vocabulary! But, if the artist never played anything but the same fugue on the same note in the same register, would he really be a composer? To compose—that is the issue.

Repetition

BL But you need to make a synthesis between our last discussion of your rapid movement from place to place (taking extremely abstract structures whose mathematical particularity is common ground for a host of objects) and the localized character that seems its complete opposite. The latter could have given us a Serres who would have been a specialist on Livy or a specialist on Lucretius or on Brillouin. I keep imagining other possible Serres . . .

MS Let's address precisely this question of the local and the global. You are defining here—through example, and without any contradictions—a certain mathematical way of thinking: formal, from the standpoint of language, using signs that tend toward the universal but immersed in a unique problem. Or take the medical way of thinking: it is supported by scientific and abstract biology but addresses itself to the singularity of a certain individual and observes the specific signs of an illness that is itself describable in general terms.

BL Biology is not a very enlightening metaphor, because, on the contrary, it gives the impression of an extremely structured metalanguage applied to a particular case. In fact, you are totally opposed to the idea of "application." If you could make an application from the general to the particular, if the text to be interpreted were no more than a specific case, this would mean that your mode of analysis would be recognizable at first glance, regardless of the subject, and that it would be equally applicable to everything.

MS You are right. I seek to avoid repetition and recognition by reiteration. Why seek recognition at any price? All or some of the problem comes from there. There is a diabolical link between repetition and recognition. The imitable is doubly ugly, especially in philosophy, because it enslaves.

BL That's a tough test if it's the one you use to distinguish a good interpretation from a bad one—since, after the first four lines, any text of yours is recognizable as being typical Serres. Not necessarily in content, but in style.

MS Thank you. A unique style comes from the gesture, the project, the itinerary, the risk—indeed, from the acceptance of a specific solitude. While using the same board, no surfer ever takes the wave in the same way, but each one accepts the eventuality of crashing beneath that unfurling wall of water or of drowning under its rolling. Repetition of content or method entails no risk, whereas style reflects in its mirror the nature of the danger. In venturing as far as possible toward nonrecognition, style runs the risk even of autism.

BL Yes, but then try to explain clearly to me what for you is a good demonstration, because the biological metaphor has not helped. You take mathematical procedure as your model, but, if there is one thing insisted on in mathematics, it's the acuity, the solidity, of both the demonstration and the discussion, conducted under the watchful eyes of colleagues. Now then, you have told us (and I am prepared to believe it) that you are obliged to add style to formalism. But where is the proof to convince us of this? You often write "QED"—"quod erat demonstrandum"—so there is obviously an exigence for proof. You don't do just anything, but the mechanism of the demonstration is hidden from the public.

MS Can we take up again the example of Pascal's *Pensées?* I've already described what I call the "fixed point" in his work. Pascal's scientific treatises are in general little algorithms; this theme brings them all together.

BL Brings them together in the sense of structure, which we talked about the other day? Do they have a common structure?

MS Variations on a common theme, to put it more simply. When you reread the *Pensées* in the light of this theme, they take on a new and classical meaning; they are illuminated. Wherever God is absent, in physical or earthly space, there is no fixed point, but nevertheless there is a fixed point on whom we can rely: Jesus Christ, who is somewhere called the center toward which all gravitates. In the first case there is neither base nor repose, as Pascal's fragment on "The Two Infinities" says. There he demonstrates that the natural world has no fixed point, whereas the supernatural world has one. We can be in repose as soon as this stable base is discovered.

BL So, for you the demonstration is made if there is a two-way trajectory, an intersection inside the text itself between the interpretive resources of the work?

MS Yes, certainly. The mathematical works, which seemed disparate, are brought together by this structure, whereas the philosophical works, themselves scattered in apparent disorder—in little thoughts comparable to the little algorithms we just mentioned—find themselves brought together in just the same way, via the same operator. Finally and consequently, the entire work becomes coherent and unique. Isn't that a convincing and rigorous demonstration?

BL But is the interpretation entirely internal, localized in the work itself?

MS We talked about it a few minutes ago. The problem—in this case the dissemination of a work—furnishes the little key (exquisitely wrought, very singular: the notion of the fixed point) that allows the problem to be resolved. This is the source of the perfect unity of a thought. Subsequently, I tried to transport this notion to neighboring philosophers, like Descartes or Leibniz, or to neighboring sciences, like the search for a center in cosmology—

but very cautiously. And that never gave as beautiful results as in the case of Pascal.

Nevertheless, this is, in fact, a demonstration, in the structuralist manner—showing that what one believed to be different is, in fact, the same thing. Finally, you have to take into account the result—order and clarity—where before had been only confusion and disorder.

Local Interpretation, Global Demonstration

BL So, this is an interpretation in the classical sense?

MS Of course, and, if you compare it to classical or contemporary interpretations, it has, further, an advantage that a mathematician would call elegance: the economical art of drawing the *maximum* number of results from a *minimum* number of suppositions. In my day what were called theoretical methods relied on a gigantic artillery of concepts so abstruse that they became more difficult than the problems they attempted to resolve and, at the end of all their labors, produced only a murky clarity. An enormous cannon/canon to budge a snail by two-thousandths of a millimeter. Here, on the contrary, is a very simple methodological structure— what could be more simple than a point, unique and fixed? It's nothing, theoretically, and yet exactly the minimal theory possible. It corresponds to a maximal clarity, a generalized coherence. A minimum of method for a maximum of results. Imagine a point, and from it you can extract a whole world.

Likewise, take Verlaine's sonnet, which I spoke of earlier. If you bring to it the theory of random noise, and the coenesthetic construction of sensory effects from background noise, the sonnet becomes absolutely luminous. Demonstration brings transparency to very dark places, like a ray of sunshine passing through a knothole.

Or take the veritably structuralist demonstration I propose for La Fontaine's fable "The Wolf and the Lamb" [in *Hermès IV. La distribution* (89–104)]. In it the intention is almost reversed, since the primary text is more transparent than a pure wave. Nonetheless, the structure of the fable's order (also very simple—in fact, none simpler—what could be easier than the sequence *before-*

after or *behind–in front?*) puts in relief a powerful and unexpected rigor. A grandiose philosophy is hidden behind the fable's feigned simplicity and naïveté. This result is in keeping with La Fontaine's intention: to put an opulent body of information in a nutshell.

In the first Hermes book, *Hermès. La communication,* there is yet another veritably classical demonstration, such as would be found in geometry or in combinatory mathematics—that of pre-established harmony, which is no doubt at the heart of Leibniz's metaphysics [154–64]. It rigorously concludes that the thesis is inevitable.

But, as far as demonstration goes, I would place above all else from that period my analogical reading of Leibniz's harmonic triangle. (He invented a triangle in the manner of Pascal, in which whole numbers are replaced by their opposites.) The challenge was to read in this table as many as possible of the author's metaphysics. It was like a musical composition on a group of organ stops—intoxicating! [see *Hermès III. La traduction* (127–33)].

In a similar fashion there is the comparison, term by term, of Lucretius' principal theses and the assembled treatises of Archimedes [in *La Naissance de la physique* (17–36)]. What joy!

Or, yet again, there is the demonstration of positivist philosophy's systematism, starting with the generalization of the famous law of the three static states—dynamic, chemical, and living—in the third Hermes book, *Hermès III. La traduction* [175–82].

Or, finally, the demonstration on whiteness, to explain with a single gesture Zola's novel *The Dream,* and which carries over to Zola's entire oeuvre [in *Feux et signaux de brume, Zola* (217–21)].

Further, it seems to me that my comparison, point by point, with no omissions, of the *Challenger* accident and the sacrifices to Baal [in *Statues* (13–34, French ed.)] is not far from being a demonstration. Do I need to add more to this list?

BL Indeed, all these examples are convincing. To return to my question of a few moments ago, we need to reconcile the need for synthesis, on one hand, and the necessity of always reforging new, localized, adapted tools. You maintain all the usual trappings of a demonstration—unity, clarity, economy, closure, saturation, synthesis—but, at the same time, just because the fixed point worked with Pascal doesn't mean it's going to work with Corneille.

MS No, of course not! That structure, the fixed point, adapts itself to Pascal, that's all. But no doubt you noticed that I didn't explain the *Pensées* from the point of view of language or of theology or of sex or economics or of the philosophy of history—in short, all the canonical approaches used elsewhere and imported there, as though one could transport them just anywhere. I read Pascal and drew from his works one specific element that is his own—this fixed point—truly invented by him but which would be worthless if applied to Malebranche or Bossuet or Corneille or Descartes.

The demonstration that is appropriate for Zola's novel would be worthless for Balzac, and the one that is appropriate for Auguste Comte would not work for Hegel. The formal gesture is always the same, but the diverse and localized elements are drawn from the area to which the demonstration is applied.

BL   Yes, but, on the contrary, in your interpretation of Verlaine's sonnet, you do in fact import noise theory?

MS No, I don't import it. Verlaine's poem springs from an authentic coenesthetic experience. The poet falls asleep and describes this falling asleep, somewhat like James Joyce at the end of *Ulysses*. And, as happens when one descends below consciousness, clouds of images appear, flecks of phosphenes, gusts of acouphenes, auditory and visible clouds that lead from the usual waking order to a sort of fluctuating disorder.

Verlaine gives equivalents to this disorder: the wasp's flight, the dancing of the specks of dust in the ray of sunlight passing through a knothole, the disorder of the wisps of hay in the stable, the sound of water falling on the ground that is being watered. Do we, as scientists, use examples other than these when we seek to explain the ordinary, clearest, precisest theories of background noise? These examples are found in scientific literature itself: the sound of falling water made by mills and by the sea. The poet's intropathic intuition easily joins our modern theories. And, in fact, the heat of our own bodies brings with it an intense background noise that we are aware of in inner experience.

From there everything becomes perfectly luminous. From this internal brouhaha everything becomes perfectly audible and sayable; language begins. Verlaine describes with great precision the same thing that it has taken us so long to learn through the sciences.

There is as much science in this poem as there is poetry, sometimes, in certain theorems. Of course, historians protest, "There was no noise theory in Verlaine's day."

BL You dismiss that completely because of "folded" time?

MS Yes. In literary works one sometimes finds perfect intuitions of scientific instruments that come later. It sometimes happens that the artist—musician, painter, poet—sees a scientific truth before it is born. Indeed, music is always in the lead: the popular saying is true, that you can't go faster than the music.

BL This is the wonderful paradox we talked about in our second conversation—that only philosophy understands why literature goes farther than philosophy.

MS Even in the sciences the imagination does the ground breaking. Do you want to talk about invention? It's impossible without that dazzling, obscure, and hard-to-define emotion called intuition. Intuition is, of all things in the world, the rarest, but most equally distributed among inventors—be they artists or scientists. Yes, intuition strikes the first blows.

BL You're saying that in this trio of literature or the arts, the sciences, and philosophy, the sciences are the latecomers, but they organize things, whereas literature is prophetic?

MS To a certain extent, often. I'm suddenly thinking of my demonstration concerning the hermaphrodite, apropos of Balzac's *Sarrasine*. It seems that no one noticed the left-right symmetrical organization in that novella. Once you grasp what crystallographers call enantiomorphism—symmetry joined to absence of left-right symmetry (discovered, you will be happy to know, in Balzac's own time)—the whole novella becomes completely luminous. And when you go back to Roland Barthes's analysis, for all its detail, it seems truly weak, for having failed to perceive this. Flawed, even, since he seems ignorant of the fact that certain castrati, far from being impotent, were reputed for their amorous exploits and, therefore, very much in demand. Even castrated dogs and cats continue to go courting on sidewalks and in gutters. Castration is not what people think it is.

BL Nonetheless, it's all very difficult to understand, to concede—your operators are always different; the demonstration is simultaneously made internally and by establishing shortcuts between vocabularies that are completely distant, exterior to the text. But is there still a principle common to all your demonstrations that allows you to decide if a given one is good or bad?

MS A method is only good if it gives good results. "By their fruits ye shall know them." Either they are beautiful, or they are dry and worthless. One tries this method and then abandons it, once it has borne fruit. Its very best fruit, of course.

I worked in that way, and then I abandoned it. I had done my share, as the saying goes.

BL Today you are no longer interested in writing commentaries on texts? You have passed from one period to another, like a painter?

MS Yes. As old age approaches, this science and all its deployments are no longer interesting. Only a certain kind of invention excites me. There is a time for abstract science and then another one for things, when you begin to think that, the more discourses are erudite and under surveillance, the less really interesting they are. There must be stages in the philosophical life—periods of abstraction and times for freedom. You draw me back to the works of my youth, which I henceforth find old, precisely because they are very learned or strictly under surveillance. Luckily, the more one writes the younger one becomes. Finally, no more surveillance; finally, I can play hooky—no more school at all.

Why don't you ask me, instead (as I would have preferred), about those things that made the philosophers decide to consider me no longer as one of their own, when I decided to free myself of parasites? Why don't you ask me about noise, about detachment, the body, the five senses, statues, death, gardens, the global Earth, the idea of the natural contract, pedagogy, the recomposition of philosophy?

BL Since the Serres of the first period was no better understood than that of the second, I'd like to continue with him. We will talk later about your reasons for abandoning textual commentary.

MS All right, against my will I'll continue where we left off, with demonstration. My demonstrations were always carried out according to the same norms but never using the same terms. In a more or less inductive way, and in contrast to unifying theories, I always started with elements that were different, drawn from the text or the problem before me, using means that were both analogous and different—a way of thinking that was both formal and relational, as I said earlier. So, I never arrived at a beginning, an origin, a unique principle of interpretation—all of which are classically seen as making coherence, system, meaning. Instead, I arrived at a cluster of relations, differentiated but organized.

BL Your work does have a synthesis, a spirit of synthesis, but there is no system, no spirit of system?

MS Yes. Synthesis, in this case, is differentiated from system or even from a methodological unity. A cluster of highly different relations becomes a body.

I'm working on a book I will describe as being on prepositions. Traditional philosophy speaks in substantives or verbs, not in terms of relationships. Thus, it always begins with a divine sun that sheds light on everything, with a beginning that will deploy itself in history (finally standardized) or with a principle—in order to deduce, through logic, a generalized logos that will confer meaning on it and establish the rules of the game for an organized debate. And, if this doesn't work, then it's great destruction, suspicion, dispersal—all the contemporary doom and gloom.

Instinctively, that's what you are asking me—that's what's always demanded from a philosopher: What is your basic substantive? Is it existence, being, language, God, economics, politics, and so on? through the whole dictionary. Where do you find meaning or rigor? Which "ism" is the name of your system? Or, worse yet, what is your obsession?

My response: I start in a dispersed way with relations, each quite different (the source of the dispersion and, interestingly, of your question), in order to end, if possible, by bringing them all together. May I point out that each of my books describes a relationship, often expressed by a unique preposition? *Inter-ference,* for the spaces and times that are *between; communication* or *contract* for the relation expressed by the preposition *with; translation* for *across;* the *para-site* for *beside* . . . and so on. *Statues* is my counter-book and asks the question: What happens in the absence of relations?

BL But this is not perceived as a method and is only recognized through style.

MS This is not perceived because the progression is inductive and always starts humbly, from the local. Because the relationship in question is not always the same. It may be left-right symmetry, the rapport maintained between the two meanings of *space* and *time/ weather.* Or noise and relational interference, or the fixed point— point of reference for relations. They always say, "But where is he?" The question assumes that the philosopher must define at the outset a grounding, a base, a principle, that he must remain fixed on a foundation. The words *substance* or *substantive* or *statute* neatly sum up these presuppositions. In fact, he must always be there, in the same place. But, as soon as you use the keys that are appropriate for the object in question, the places necessarily differ. So, I wander. I let myself be led by fluctuations. I follow the relations and will soon regroup them, just as language regroups them via prepositions.

BL Wait—this sheds some light on things. If you have no fixed metalanguage (since each time it is the object that gives it to you), there is nonetheless one that is your own?

MS Yes.

BL The terms defining this metalanguage will be different each time, since they are drawn either from the scientific repertoire brought to bear on the literary intuition or, on the contrary, from the artistic work itself . . .

MS Both. The operator is extracted from the work, and the way it is used follows the norms of mathematical demonstration.

BL And the word topology *can describe this meta-metalanguage?*

MS No, *topology* only describes the freedom I take with ordinary metric theory—with the usual theory of space and time. For example, folded, crumpled time, which we talked about at great length, and about which I hope to write a book. Time is the presupposition of the entire question.

   More generally, the whole set of relations—no doubt fuzzy—is its largest presupposition.

BL Yes, I understood that. The ontology of time defines your way of moving from place to place.

MS I'm not so sure that ontology is the name for the philosophical discipline concerned with the whole set of relations. Or, rather, I'm sure it's not.

BL But I'm trying to understand the rapport between the need to reforge explanatory concepts locally and, at the same time, the need for a synthesis that will have nothing to do with content, with the repetition of a certain language, but, rather, with a certain way of moving from place to place. The synthesis is going to come from this way of moving. If I understand you, the metalanguage is always different, and this is what distances you from the dominant, domineering philosophy . . .

MS That's it, exactly. Relations are, in fact, ways of moving from place to place, or of wandering.

BL But above these ever-changing metalanguages there is still a meta-metalanguage, if we can call it that, which itself remains relatively stable, since you were even speaking of "norms." It is not defined by certain words or certain concepts but, rather, by a mode of moving from place to place. Is it this highly recognizable, identifiable mode that allows you to say whether an interpretation is right or not? If a demonstration is finished or not? Is this your superego, in a way?

MS More my mode of abstraction. To talk only by means of substantives or verbs, and thus to write in a telegraphic code, as ordinary philosophy does, defines a different form of abstraction from the one I propose, which relies on prepositions.

The Second Period: Movement instead of Textual Commentary

BL All this has shed light on your first period, that of your scientific youth and your textual commentaries. Several years ago you abandoned commentary and passed on to things. Can you define this move, which in a painter would be called a new period?

MS We're on that track. Now let's forget content—science, literature, anthropology, even the content of philosophy. There are simply bodies of texts, situations, places, objects. Fewer and fewer texts, too, and more and more objects. Statues, sensations, as in *Les Cinq sens* [The Five Senses], or much larger objects, like the Earth, in *The Natural Contract.* Let's try to forget that there are distinct disciplines—literature, the arts, etc. Let's try to see that the mode of moving from place to place is the scientific mode. Science is not a content but, rather, a means of getting about.

I will go back, if it's possible to say so, to my next book. We are used to abstracting according to a certain style or type of abstraction, generally based on verbs or substantives: *the being,* or *I think, causality, freedom, essence, existence, immanence, transcendence,* and so on. Verbs or substantives—that's been the mode of abstraction from Plato to Heidegger. The philosophical concept par excellence is enunciated by means of a substantive or a verb.

BL Enunciation meaning postulation, not expression.

MS To wit, the titles of my books: *Interférence, Traduction, Passage du Nord-Ouest, Feux et signaux de brume* [Interference, Translation, The Northwest Passage, Lighthouses and Fog Horns]. Their type of abstraction takes place in the movement from place to place. I even place the book on lighthouses not far from the one on the Northwest Passage! From a distance this seems difficult to understand, but from close up, it's a very simple matter. As simple as saying hello. In fact, we say hello to passersby, to people we encounter in our movements from place to place.

So, I don't make my abstractions starting from some *thing* or some *operation,* but *throughout* a relation, a rapport. A reading of my books may seem difficult, because it changes and moves all the time. This changing, these transformations, wanderings, crisscrossings, in each trip follow or invent the path of a relation. Even my book on the hermaphrodite [*L'Hermaphrodite: Sarrasine sculpteur*] deploys a kind of relation, in which the male and the female are not considered so much as is the relation that unites them in closest proximity and the close rapport between right and left.

Thus, one must seize the gesture as the relation is in progress and prolong it. There is neither beginning nor end; there is a sort of vector. That's it—I think vectorially. Vector: vehicle, sense, direction, the trajectory of time, the index of movement or of transformation. Thus, each gesture is different, obviously.

BL So, it's no longer a question of circulating among texts, as in your first period, but of taking circulation among things as an object in itself?

MS The abstraction itself that I have in view (and that I was not looking for when I began) is not so much in place as circulating. My effort consists of abstracting, throughout the duration of relations, the different mailmen or messengers—represented by the god Hermes or the host of angels—who serve as delivery persons for prepositions. This is the reason for my attraction to topology—the science of proximities and ongoing or interrupted transformations—and my attraction to percolation theory and to the notion of mixture.

A verb or a substantive chosen from the galaxy of Ideas, from the categories either in consciousness or in the subject, spawns systems or histories that are static, even if they claim to describe a process of becoming. It's better to paint a sort of fluctuating picture of relations and rapports—like the percolating basin of a glacial river, unceasingly changing its bed and showing an admirable network of forks, some of which freeze or silt up, while others open up—or like a cloud of angels that passes, or the list of prepositions, or the dance of flames.

I want to finish drawing this navigational map, this inventory—fluctuating and mobile—before I die. Once this work is done it will be clearly seen that all the rapports I traced out either followed or invented a possible road across the ensemble of movements from place to place. Note that this maritime chart, an ocean of possible routes, fluctuates and does not remain static like a map. Each route invents itself.

BL   Wait. Is this a road on the map or a way of tracing different roads? Your argument on enunciation, on prepositions, has implications not just for networks but for the ways to trace these networks.

MS Yes.

BL   Tracings, not tracks.

MS Pre-positions—what better name for those relations that precede any position?

Imagine dancing flames. As I write this new book, I have before my eyes this crimson curtain that fluctuates, sends up great shoots, disappears, is fragmented, invades and illuminates space, only to die out, suddenly, in darkness. It is a complex and supple network, never in equilibrium—in other words, "existing"—striking and fluctuating swiftly in time, and having ill-defined edges.

BL So, there is in this new period a different way of abstracting?

MS Instead of creating an abstraction based on substantives—that is, on concepts or verbs (meaning on operations)—or even from adverbs or adjectives modifying the substantive or the verb, I abstract *toward, by, for, from,* and so on, down the list of prepositions. I follow them the way one follows a direction: one takes it and then abandons it. It's as though the wise grammarian who named them "prepositions" knew that they preceded any possible position. Once I have worked out the maritime map of these spaces and times that precede any thesis (meaning position), I can die. I will have done my work.

Do you notice that, in relation to other parts of speech, the preposition has almost all meaning and has almost none? It simultaneously has the maximum and minimum of meaning, exactly like a variable in classical analysis. *From*—the French *de*—indicates origin, attribution, cause, and thus almost anything one wishes; this is the word that is demonstrably the most used in the French language and that reveals its status as a noble language! The path traced by this rapport starts everywhere and goes almost everywhere; like Hermes, it passes, and only passes. Likewise, the prepositions *to* or *by* denote ways of tracing relations more than they fix the outlines of these relations. A verb or a substantive would fix them.

Consider the "post-positions" in the English language. The verb they gravitate around is like an empty face, around which agitates this great mane of possibilities. You add *up, down, in,* or *over* around it, like strands of hair that blow in all directions—like dancing limbs, valences, flames, seaweed, or banners.

BL But this assumes a different definition of the map of knowledge. Just as your conception of time explained a lot of problems encountered in reading works from your first period, couldn't we say that your second period is clarified by your conception of the map of relationships?

MS Do you remember that we said earlier that the classification of knowledge was in the process of changing, that its landscape was being modified? That the very concept we had of it was being transformed, globally?

BL So, comprehension is entirely different under those two definitions of encyclopedism?

MS Certainly. One last word on the difficulty of *comprehending*. As we know, this verb signifies "to hold together." A single building holds together its stones, which don't move. What a simple and lazy way to "comprehend"! In order to understand, nothing must move, like an assemblage of stupid, dark stones, which always maintain among themselves the same relation of fixed metrical distance.

Lucretius launches us into movement—everything in his work begins with turbulence—it's a very complex figure, which you call difficult. Nonetheless, if you follow his vortices, they bring things together, forming and destroying worlds, bodies, souls, knowledge, etc. Turbulence isn't a system, because its constituents fluctuate, fluid and mobile. Rather, it is a sort of confluence, a form in which fluxes and fluctuation enter, dance, crisscross, making together the sum and the difference, the product and the bifurcation, traversing scales of dimension. It recruits at the very heart of chaos by ceaselessly inventing different relations; it returns to it as well.

A viscosity takes over. It comprehends. It creates comprehension. It teaches. But one must concede that everything is not solid and fixed and that the hardest solids are only fluids that are slightly more viscous than others. And that edges and boundaries are fluctuating. Fluctuating fluid. Then intelligence enters into time, into the most rapid, lively, and subtle shifts and fluctuations of turbulence, of the dancing flames. Yes, it is an advancement in the very notion of comprehension. Relations spawn objects, beings and acts, not vice versa.

So—stand up, run, jump, move, dance! Like the body, the mind needs movement, especially subtle and complex movement.

A Synthesis Based on Relations

BL In this new period do you still retain something from the sciences, or have you swung completely away from them?

MS My way of abstracting is still not so far from that of certain very contemporary sciences, and perhaps generalizes them, in the sense that, in mathematics, for example, and even sometimes in physics, relations outnumber subjects or objects.

Just as Leibniz wrote a monadology, an elementary or atomic philosophy, here is a theory of valences around atoms, a general theory of relations, like a theology in which the important thing would be angelology—a turbulent array of messengers.

BL Wait a minute. This is very important, but I'm lost again. You're taking up again the metaphor of scientific method, which will not completely convince me, since, on the contrary, the general impression is that the sciences are multiple substantives, a formidable proliferation of objects, whereas for you the synthesizing element . . .

MS . . . is relations.

BL But, even more than relations, the types of relation.

MS Not only the mode of relation but the way this mode of relation establishes or invents itself, virtually or physically.

BL Is it like comparing passes in rugby? I mean the ways of passing and not the configurations of the players?

MS Configurations or fixed places are important when the players don't move—just before the game begins, or when certain established positions are called for at various points in the game— scrimmages or line-outs. They begin to fluctuate as soon as the game begins, and the multiple and fluctuating ways of passing the ball are traced out.

The ball is played, and the teams place themselves in relation to it, not vice versa. As a quasi object, the ball is the true subject of the game. It is like a tracker of the relations in the fluctuating collectivity around it. The same analysis is valid for the individual: the clumsy person plays with the ball and makes it gravitate around himself; the mean player imagines himself to be a subject by imagining the ball to be an object—the sign of a bad philosopher. On the contrary, the skilled player knows that the ball plays with him or plays off him, in such a way that he gravitates around it and fluidly follows the positions it takes, but especially the relations that it spawns.

BL So, your synthesis would come about in the area of the passes, of movement, and not in the area of the objects?

MS Look at how the flames dance, where they go, from whence they come, toward what emptiness they head, how they become fragmented and then join together or die out. Both fluctuating and dancing, this sheet of flame traces relations. This is an illuminating metaphor, if I may say so, for understanding what I have in view—this continuing and fragmented topological variety, which outlines crests, which can shoot high and go out in a moment. The flames trace and compose these relations.

BL Wait, I need to back up a minute. I thought I understood that there was in general a hermetical conception . . .

MS Hermes passes and disappears; makes sense and destroys it; exposes the noise, the message, and the language; invents writing and, before it, music, translations and their obstacles. He is admittedly not a fixed preposition but, as is said nowadays about mailmen, he plays at *pré-posé*, at delivery person.

BL There is a first Hermes operator that establishes rapprochements, ties between vocabularies and objects that appear quite distant, but that you see as close, because of folded time. Let's say that this Hermes traces networks. You have defined this operator a thousand times. It's your metalanguage, but it is never recognized as a metalanguage because it's never defined twice in the same way, and it changes in each setting. This is the source of your criticism of philosophy, of "bad" abstraction, of the separation between science and the humanities, etc. Then there is a second operator, in some sense above the first. The one you're now talking about in your new book, which, for the first time, will produce a synthesis. But it can't be defined by concepts, it's what I call a meta-metalanguage—not because it's indefinable or ineffable, not because it's always changing, but because it defines ways of passing, passes. Now you're saying that it's possible to make a synthesis of these modes of passing.

MS A synthesis only in the sense I've just described.

BL You're able to produce the grammar of these modes, which should not be infinite in number . . .

MS . . . although one must be wary of the spatial image. Networks, even if you add the idea of virtual modes of tracing, leave an image in space that is almost too stable. But, if you immerse it in time, this network itself is going to fluctuate, become very unstable, and bifurcate endlessly.

This is why I use examples of turbulences in fluid, liquid or air—and, now, these flames. I should perhaps choose other examples, in music. The kinds of relations that are constructed change. All of this led me to questions of noise, disorder, and chaos in the mid-1970s, when I was writing *Lucrèce, Distribution, Passage,* and this *Genesis*—"Noise."

BL   So, for you there is a bad philosophical abstraction, having to do, let's say, with postulates. For classical philosophers the goal is to master postulation, to choose among all postulates the one that will represent all the others—for example, existence . . .

MS   Yes—although "bad" is putting it somewhat strongly. Being, essence, consciousness, matter—all these things seem like fetishes to me now. Like statues. Indeed, these concepts that ape comprehension more than they invent or nurture it seem to belong to an age of fetishism or philosophical polytheism. They are like painted plaster statues. But I openly admit my inexcusable weakness for polytheism and statues.

BL   You're defining metaphysics by postulates. Whereas you yourself are fully in favor of abstraction, of synthesis, of argumentation, but you lean toward the side of relations, of systems of expression that allow for the production of all possible expositions.

MS   Exactly.

Hermes as Dispersion and Synthesis

BL   So, there are two levels. On the first Hermes introduces confusion in philosophers' postulates. On the second he reintroduces order, differentiation. Is it the same Hermes who wreaks havoc and who re-establishes order, who makes the synthesis?

MS   Do you mean "wreaks havoc" or "verges on chaos"? In the first case a few pupils make an uproar in the teacher's classroom, like the surrealists. But in the second case we follow in the footsteps of some pre-Socratics and several empiricists.

I have never abandoned Hermes, who constitutes the unity of my work. Even his caduceus, as a kind of vortex, embodies a preposition, *toward* (French *vers*), pointing out a direction with its axis. But its Latin root, *versus* (from *vertere*, to turn), imposes the snakes that are twined around it. Circulating and hastening toward his destination, Hermes holds in his hand his own emblem, the preposition *toward* (*vers*), which simultaneously describes a translation and a system of rotations, a helix or a vortex. . . . *Se non è vero, è ben trovato!*

BL So, it is in fact always the same Hermes?

MS Yes. The kind of unity or abstraction at which I aim has never abandoned him, because of his role, his wanderings, his inventions and movements. Thanks in part to him, the unifying and synthesizing impulse never abandons local, radical pluralism. He passes everywhere, visiting places in their specific detail and their singularity.

The possibility for synthesis was really there, from the beginning. If I had it to do over, I would probably go through the same stages. *Amor fati!* Everything that happens is admirable, except that I would have liked to have done better—in quality, beauty, serenity.

BL So, if you are not recognized as having carried out synthesizing demonstrations, it's because . . .

MS . . . it's very difficult. When you are working on relationships that are in process, you're like a man who takes a plane from Toulouse to Madrid, travels by car from Geneva to Lausanne, goes on foot from Paris toward the Chevreuse Valley, or from Cervina to the top of the Matterhorn (with spikes on his shoes, a rope and an ice ax), who goes by boat from Le Havre to New York, who swims from Calais to Dover, who travels by rocket toward the moon, travels by semaphore, telephone or fax, by diaries from childhood to old age, by monuments from antiquity to the present, by lightning bolts when in love. One may well ask, "What in the world is that man doing?"

There are differences in the mode of traveling, the reason for the trip, the point of departure and the destination, in the places through which one will pass, the speed, the means, the vehicle, the obstacles to be overcome, in what space and time. And, since I have used diverse methods, the coherence of my project is suspect. In fact, I have always analyzed the mode of travel in my movements from place to place. Admittedly, the differentiation of gestures and operations can make things difficult, but, in fact, it was always a matter of establishing a relation, constructing it, fine-tuning it. And once established, thousands of relations, here, there, everywhere—after a while, when you step back and look, a picture emerges. Or at least a map. You see a general theory of relations, without any point focalizing the construction or solidifying it, like a pyramid. The turbulences keep moving; the flames keep dancing.

BL That's the problem.

MS No doubt. We are accustomed to abstraction via concepts, to concepts from one area organizing the totality of everything. Which explains the smugness surrounding those who continually repeat "the ontology of Being," "Ideas," or "categories," with references to the "knowing subject," "the analysis of language," and so on—as though it were always a matter of constructing (or tearing down) a very solid edifice, whose peak or foundation would organize all stability.

It's possible to compose outside of solidity—in fuzziness and fluctuation. Nature itself does nothing else, or almost!

BL Except that all the great philosophers have tried, like you, to understand this relationship.

MS Do you think so? Leibniz, indeed, at the end of his life, ended with a theory of the vinculum, a theory of this relation I'm seeking to describe. In his letters to des Bosses he puts the final touches on his theory of that link, which has been aptly translated into French by Christiane Frémont as the "*lien substantiel*," the link of substantiality. But precisely, as she demonstrates in her excellent book, the link "substantiates": it produces substance. In the final analysis everything comes back to the substantive—even relations.

BL What about Hegel? What about all the philosophers who fought against essence with the same argument?

MS They replaced it with existence. A very tiny sidestep from the status quo, not amounting to a gigantic move. As far as I know, relations in Hegel are not very numerous or very pliable.

BL What about Heidegger? What about the argument that all philosophy has never addressed anything but metaphysics and that it should lean toward the production of all possible metaphysics?

MS Perhaps. Again, I repeat that I never claim to be doing anything exceptional but, rather, to be working in the direct line of philosophical tradition.

BL We'll get back to philosophical tradition next time. But, in general, it's your way of conceiving abstraction that makes your work difficult to read. Your abstractions are just that, but they are unrelated to any existing hypotheses. You want to leap over the level of metalanguage, leaving it to the local, to risk, to chaos, to fluctuation, and to make your synthesis on the basis of modes of relation.

MS Yes, modes. By a theory of modality, of means, of relations, of rapports, of transports, of wandering. Isn't that, overall, a contemporary manner of thinking? For example, aren't physicists seeking to understand interactions in general?

BL Yes, but their metalanguage organizes, is imperialistic—exactly the opposite of what you are seeking.

MS No doubt. But I am not seeking wholeheartedly to imitate scientific methods. As neither mistress nor servant, philosophy seeks aids, adjuncts, values, wherever they may be found, while remaining independent.

BL I'm not sure the sciences are that useful to us, since there are a thousand ways to approach the sciences, and you yourself always approach them in a very particular way. You never take on "Big Science"; you always address the theory, never, for example, the experiment. You leave the experimental sciences absolutely alone. You only take from the sciences that aspect of them that is already very philosophical—theories that have been purified to the limit, filtered, mathematicized. Further, you never take anything but the great results, never the process of production, never the laboratory, never the real work.

MS The real work? At first glance, you seem right. But I abandoned epistemology as well. And these scientific methods serve me more as checks than as models. I mean by this that I am seeking compatibility more than imitation.

Nonetheless, exactitude and rigor remain indispensable and common to all acts of disciplined thought, as well as a certain faithfulness to the state of things. In the arts, also. From this springs what I call compatibility. We live in the same world—that of the intellectually curious.

BL So, you are in fact a rationalist, but you practice a rationalism that is in some way generalized. What you imitate is not the idea we have of the sciences but, rather, the new forms of organization they propose?

MS Yes. The conception, the construction, the production of rapports, of relations, of transports—communication in general—evolve so fast that they continually construct a new world, in real time. We still live in a century or a universe of concepts, beings, objects, archaic statues, or even operators, while we continually produce an environment of fluctuating interferences, which in return produce us.

Hermes, by renewing himself, becomes continuously our new god, for as long as we've been humans—not only the god of our ideas or our behavior, of our theoretical abstractions, but also the god of our works, of our technology, of our experiments, of our experimental sciences. Indeed, he is the god of our laboratories, where, as you have pointed out, everything functions through networks of complex relations between messages and people. He is the god of our biology, which describes messages transmitted by the central nervous system or by genetics. He is the god of computer science, of rapid finance and volatile money, of commerce, of information, of the medias which produce a third reality, independent of the one we hold as real. He's the god of the rapports between the law and science. In short, suddenly here I am in Big Science, which is itself immersed in contemporary conditions and is immersing those conditions in itself—that Big Science you just reproached me for not addressing. As far as I can tell, you are trying, as I am, to construct a philosophy that is compatible with this new world. Not in order to imitate it, nor to justify it, but in order to understand it, and, desperately, perhaps, to know how—to be able—to direct its course. For the first time in history we think it really depends on us.

BL And Hermes is the philosophy associated with this?

MS Hermes comprehends it—through his role, his figure, and his movements—but curiously, as a person and not as a concept, as a multiple and continuous transport, and not as a foundation or a starting point. We have to imagine a foundation with wings on its feet! A person who is talked about more than he is deduced. His movements and travels from place to place can be sketched more easily than constructed. Thanks to him, I attempt to explain my own movements in narrative form. Beyond localized, rigorous, and regulated explications, there is a mobile globality that is often better expressed by narrative than by any theory.

Thus, I finish *The Natural Contract* with a series of narratives on the bond, the cord, the relation, the tie that is knotted or undone (which is implied by every contract), by little tales and short stories that jump, like Hermes, from bond to bond and from tied knots to denouements. This mixture is very distasteful to some people and sometimes exposes me to misunderstanding. But, as I have said before, this is so traditional in philosophy that Aristotle himself wrote that he who tells stories is engaging in a way in philosophy, just as he who philosophizes in some sense tells stories.

You will say, rightly, that Aristotle justifies nothing and does not constitute an argument. I will reply that my goal is not above all to be right but, rather, to produce a global intuition, profound and sensible.

BL Perhaps I am, in fact, too relentless. But, to continue, so it is narration alone that allows this intuition?

MS Let's go back to the example of the apologues or parables that end *The Natural Contract.* Solidary humanity faces up to a global Earth, in three systems of unbalanced relations: those new ones linking mankind, those composing terraqueous globality based on localities, and, finally, those linking these two networks. Humanity floats like a fetus in amniotic fluid, linked by a thousand ties to mother Earth. Then the story stops and inverts the relationship: Earth itself floats like a fetus, linked by all possible relations to mother Science. And, in the earthquake at the end, the narrator, who appears in person, seems to make love to Earth, in this new relationship, or disorder, that is dangerous, moving, and vibrant.

So, in the balance, Earth is mother then daughter and, finally, lover. Humanity collectively enters into this fluctuating relationship, as daughter then as mother and, finally, in amorous desire. When relationships remain sane or normal, they fluctuate this way; only fixed and frozen relationships are pathogenic. What better way to describe this fluctuation than with everyday words, concrete experiences—in short, by narrative?

I had to describe global relations that are as fluctuating as those in turbulence, in my attempt to discern what is transcendental in contractual and vital global relations, under what conditions the widest relationality is possibile.

From this emerges a global object: Earth. On the other hand, a global subject takes shape. It remains for us to understand the global relations between these two globalities. But we still have no theory that allows us to do this. So, I see myself as forced to narrate the progressive construction of this thought—beginning, quasi-mythologically, with Adam and Eve, brought together and separated; then by stitching together, piece by piece, like a harlequin's patchwork cape, small communities, a roped party tied and undone, a ship, a family, all the way to total integration, just as in the past I assembled, detail by detail, the outline of Hermes's activities. Rarely additive, this stitching together of the pieces once again resembles the Northwest Passage.

The Synthesis of Hermes and Angels

BL Why can't Hermes's activity be seen directly? Because we can only see its traces?

MS It constructs itself, it creates itself, following the fluctuations of time. It could only be sketched out at the risk of freezing it once again into statuelike concepts, operations, or verbs, too simplistic and coarse.

BL This is where your scientific metaphor doesn't work too well. Because if there's one thing scientists know very well how to construct, it's that very statue. And that control, that domination, that mastery. Here you are talking, on the contrary, of objects that are behind you, that are never in front of you, that are not objects to be mastered and yet which will serve you in making your demonstration.

MS Perhaps. When I describe the dance of the flames or the system of relations between us and the global Earth, I aim at the transcendental in those relations.

BL Yes, but Hermes, in the preceding interpretation—that of networks—is nonetheless a restless figure. He himself is not differentiated. A person

*could read your works and say that Hermes is a rover, unsystematic, a
tourist, a dabbler.*

MS Restless, in order to go everywhere, throughout the entire
encyclopedia—what an undertaking! Restless—in other words, active, not lazy. Unsystematic, in order to criticize outdated systems.
To show, with a laugh, that the space of knowledge has changed
its contours and that these are more tortuous than we realize.
Unsystematic—that is to say, fertilely inventive in the middle of
chaos. This is where we get the name Plato gave to the father of
love, Poros—resourceful, or, in nobler terms, expedient. Hermes
is worse than a tourist; he is a miserable wanderer, crossing the
desert. And, worse yet, he's a troublemaker. Even a thief, if you
will! He's both good and bad. And hermetical, in the bargain. Do
you find this terrible? I imagine Hermes as filled with joy.

And something that's even more interesting: Hermes is the one
who invented the nine-stringed lyre. What is a musical instrument,
if not a table on which one can compose a thousand languages,
and as many melodies and chants? Its invention opens the way for
an infinite number of inventions. This is good philosophy in action, whose excellent goal is to invent the transcendental space,
the conditions, for possible inventions of the future. The invention of possible inventions. This is a good image, followed by a
good generalization, of what I was pointing out a little while ago:
the conditional space and time for transporting messages back
and forth. So, touch all the strings of this instrument and compose
at leisure the possible ballads: this opens up a whole time.

The character of Hermes is henceforth complete. Universal
and unique, concrete and abstract, formal, transcendental, and
narratable.

*BL Yes, except that your new synthesizing argument gives him another
quality that is not in the mythology: Hermes becomes capable of defining
his own modes of travel.*

MS What makes you think he could not do this before? What
supergod told you that a god could find himself limited in this
way?

*BL Your transcendental Hermes is someone who reflects and would be
capable of classifying his modes of travel. This seems contradictory, especially when you claim to imitate scientific coherence, based on a theory of*

relationships, and at the same time you do not want anything to dominate, you do not want a stable or calculated conceptualization of these relations, which must, on the contrary, be sensed, not understood.

MS It's possible to sketch a global landscape without classifying. Do you believe that classifying is a highly philosophical operation? It presupposes exclusion, and the excluded middle third. No doubt we'll get back later to this "third" beast, whose portrait comes up often, from *L'Hermaphrodite* to *Le Tiers-Instruit*.

Today what comes up even more than the figure of Hermes is the figure he will take on at his death—or, rather, the figure that comes at the death of his father, Pan, at the beginning of the Christian era, taking into account Semitic influences—that of the multiplicity of angels. There are, in fact, classes of angels, and the multiplicity of these messengers fills the heavens. Have you seen in Rome those reredos whose backgrounds are filled with wings?

Traditional philosophy usually has either a central god who is a producer, a radiating source of life like a sun, or a story of the origin of time. My philosophy is more like a heaven filled with angels, obscuring God somewhat. They are restless, unsystematic (which you find suspect), troublemakers, boisterous, always transmitting, not easily classifiable, since they fluctuate. Making noise, carrying messages, playing music, tracing paths, changing paths, carrying . . .

BL *Holy Virgins in assumption* . . .

MS The Holy Virgin, saints, popes, all of society and what it produces, like elevators! Hiding God, revealing God. This is the transcendental I'm talking about—the archangelic space-time, the enormous cloud, without clear edges, of angels who pass, a great turbulence of passages. A swarm. Perhaps what I was writing all along was an angelology.

BL *This is not going to clarify things for the public. You are supposed to be offering us clarifications here!*

MS It's not clear? You astonish me! What could be more luminous than a space traversed with messages? Look at the sky, even right here above us. It's traversed by planes, satellites, electromagnetic waves from television, radio, fax, electronic mail. The world we are immersed in is a space-time of communication. Why shouldn't I call it angel space, since this means the messengers, the systems of mailmen, of transmissions in the act of passing or the space through which they pass? Do you know, for example, that at every moment there are at least a million people on flights through the sky, as though immobile or suspended—nonvariables with variations? Indeed, we live in the century of angels.

BL I must disagree. I'm fond of angels, but I don't believe that they are in the least like Hermes. I believe that the error lies in communication, in the modes of travel. Angels don't travel like Hermes.

MS Theologians and some philosophers used to say, not unreasonably, that they arrived somewhere the moment they thought about going there; thus, they traveled at the speed of thought. For some people, at least, this is fast enough.

BL I don't believe in it, because they don't have any messages to transport. But it's not important—this is a theological quarrel!

MS The angels are the messages; their very body is a message. But what differentiates angels from Hermes is their multiplicity, their cloud, their whirlwinds. I was about to say their chaos, since their collectivity is similar to it. In the reredos in Rome sometimes there are ninety-seven of them, sometimes thirty-two, sometimes twelve—why these numbers? Pure multiplicity.

Further, we're talking about delivery people, relational bodies. I imagine that for every angel there is a corresponding preposition. But a preposition does not transport messages; it indicates a network of possible paths, either in space or in time.

In Praise of Fragile Synthesis, Rather than Fragmentation

BL I would like to end this conversation on demonstration with a point you alluded to a while ago, in speaking of a necessary synthesis. Contemporary philosophies have swung away from systematic philosophies, toward philosophies of fragmentation. But your interest in localized phenomena, your systematic destruction of the metalanguages of essence or existence, have not resulted in praise for the fragmentary, for the localized itself. You share with traditional philosophy the will to synthesis. Thus, you are outside of both forms of philosophy. You are against philosophies with a

*single center, with a Copernican revolution around a central God—but
you are also against those that delight in the singular...*

MS ...locality. Yes, criticism, destruction, pieces or disparate
body parts weigh on me. I have seen enough of them in ditches,
swimming in blood, in my youth. The horizon of the war is always
there behind me, moving me, propelling me.

And what if we learn a bit about the mechanics of materials?
These show us that a philosophy of the fragmentary is conservative. Why? Let's take a vase or some object that is more solid, more
constructed, larger. The larger it is, the more fragile it is. If you
break it, the smaller the fragment is, the more resistant it is. Consequently, when you create a fragment, you seek refuge in places,
in localities, which are more resistant than a global construction.
The destroyer himself fears destruction, since he can only keep
what is least destructible. In the end the particle is indivisible; the
element is invincible—united, as we know, by an enormous force.
So, the philosophy of fragments is hyperdefensive; it is the result
of hypercriticism, of polemics, of battle and hatred. It produces
what is the most resistant to the strongest aggression. The atom
produces the atomic bomb, whose power protects against itself.

Inversely, to construct on a large scale is to move in the direction of fragility, to accept it, to run its risk. To move in the direction of the fragment is the same as to protect oneself. The philosophy of fragments is a by-product of war but equally a technique
of conservation. Museums are stuffed with bits and pieces, with
disparate members. The philosophy of fragments brings together
the philosophy of the museum and the museum of philosophy;
thus, it is doubly conservative.

Constructing on a large scale means moving toward vulnerabil-
ity; thus, synthesis requires courage—the audacity of the frail. Contrary to popular belief, the largest things are fragile, especially
organic things. I would like to make a construction at the limits
of fragility, since relations are sometimes extremely labile, extremely unstable, often living or turbulent like breaths of wind—
perhaps spiritual?—and thus much frailer than the stable pyramids generally constructed by architectonic metaphysics and
assumed by destructive criticism. This is the same kind of logic and

solidity found in the great visions of history, in a pseudotime. How easy it is to destroy something rigid!

BL So your criticism of the architectonic is not because it seeks a large scale but because it seeks this largeness through a construction favoring postulates? All of your antisystematic arguments are not arguments against a large scale, against systematic character?

MS No. I love great size—grandeur. It also epitomizes what is ethical and—why not?—what is aesthetic. There is no such thing as the attractive and the unattractive, the beautiful and the ugly: there are large scales and small scales. Thus, the frail component and the sparse fragments. A fragile peace for a thousand solid wars!

BL There has to be a system.

MS Does there? I don't know, but philosophy would not be worth anything if it remained fragmentary. Hard and small. In the etymological sense, *minable*—worthless.

BL Do you dismiss entirely the clichés about the end of the great philosophical systems?

MS When everyone around you is demonstrating that no one can walk, it's a good time to get up quickly and start running. As quickly as Hermes or the angels.

The system's "matter" has changed "phase," at least since Bergson. It's more liquid than solid, more airlike than liquid, more informational than material. The global is fleeing toward the fragile, the weightless, the living, the breathing—perhaps toward the spirit?

Indeed, the flames' dance takes strength from its lightness. All the nonsolid bodies have taken the part of weakness. And a lot more can be accomplished with this than with force or hardness. The gentle lasts longer than the hard. Absolutely! Great evolutions come about thanks to failures, even—perhaps especially—Darwinian evolution, and no doubt all of those in history. Allow me to say that what drives history is, precisely, failures. Don't forget, please, to include among "failures" the poor, the excluded, and the most miserable. I even believe that, among the attributes of God, the theologians have forgotten infinite weakness. Could God be "nilpotent" rather than omnipotent?

As for history, it advances and retreats at a shuffle, like an invalid. Humanity makes progress most often thanks to small children, women, old people, the sick, the simpleminded, and the poorest. Our flesh is weak, our spirit is frail, and our advances are fragile, our relations remain unspoken, our works are made of flesh, of words and of wind.... And everything else deafens, through the publicity of the strong, who believe they make and do everything, while all they really make is war—death and destruction, the return to fragments. These are the adults who seek the fragmentary and deadly explosive force of atoms.

Everything that is solid, crystalline, strong, that flaunts its hardness, that seeks to resist—from crustaceans to breastplates, statues and walls, saber-rattling military types, mechanical assemblages with nuts and bolts—all of that is irrevocably archaic and frozen. Like dinosaurs. Whereas fluids, most living things, communications, relations—none of that is hard. Fragile, vulnerable, fluid, ready to fade away with the first breath of wind. Ready to vanish, to return to nothingness. Nature is born, is going to be born, gets ready to be born, like a fragile infant.

BL So, you're seeking a synthesis of fragility?

MS What I seek to form, to compose, to promote—I can't quite find the right word—is a *syrrhèse*, a confluence not a system, a mobile confluence of fluxes. Turbulences, overlapping cyclones and anticyclones, like on the weather map. Wisps of hay tied in knots. An assembly of relations. Clouds of angels passing. Once again, the flames' dance. The living body dances like that, and all life. Weakness and fragility mark the spot of their most precious secret. I seek to assist the birth of an infant.

Mankind is the mother of all weaknesses. The word springs from the birth wail, life springs from chance encounters, thought comes from a momentary fluctuation, science comes from an intuition that clicks and then vanishes instantly. Life and thought live in closest proximity to nothingness. Even more so does man when he approaches weakness—woman, child, old person, the sick, the mad, the poor, the indigent, the hungry, the miserable.

This is where the third, the excluded middle, reappears—through the servants' entrance, pitiful and unrecognizable. So, this is a philosophy for the third and the fourth worlds. These poorest worlds have more to do with our future than does the rich West, with its atomic shields and its aircraft carriers that no longer serve except to kill the wretched. The sated sleep in the shadow of their armaments, while the most fragile are bringing grandeur and newness.

The End of Criticism

Bruno Latour: In our preceding conversations we raised some difficulties encountered in reading your works. Your triple passage, from traditional science to revolutionary science, from the sciences to philosophy, then from traditional philosophy to literature and mythology, has made you lose your masters and your disciples. You have lost them along the way. In our second conversation we addressed (definitively, I hope) the ridiculous accusation (or would-be praise, which is even worse) that you "write in poetry," that you "write well but are obscure." You make your relationships through contemporary mathematical procedures, but your domain of comparison is so vast that you must seek recourse not in formalism but in style. It's in transforming and honing spoken language that you make it as precise as formalism. For you, style serves your generalized comparativism, your generalized rationalism, your rigorous demonstrations.

Michel Serres: When it's reduced to mere ornamentation, style vanishes. To what does it add? Style reveals methodology. Even in mathematics G. G. Granger was able to define a vectorial style in the work of Grassman, another style in the work of Euclid, and so on. The rigor of French classical writers and their insistence on algebraic precision are conveyed by perfect form, which makes La Fontaine's fables almost like theorems or Corneille's tragedies veritable treatises on political anthropology or law—and less boring. Philosophers invent words, a syntax, and even literary forms, like the dialogue, the essay, the meditation, the ramble . . .

BL We have already talked about the question of learned ignorance and your ambivalence toward the world of erudition.

MS Can we say that knowledge has two modes? The concern with verification and the burdens it requires, but also risk taking, the production of newness, the multiplicity of found objects—in short, inventiveness.

It's better to avoid diminishing the second aspect in favor of the first. Begin with one, continue with the other. That way the movement depends only on itself, and language on language; this is the hour of a style that is linked, lightly, at its crest, to the water of the wave created by style. In a whirlpool, a waterspout. It unfurls. This is where invention springs from, like Aphrodite, newborn, standing on the waves.

BL In our discussions we moved on to try to shed light on something more difficult. We addressed the accusation (and here again, praise would be worse) of "dabbling in everything." We defined your desire for synthesis, but this synthesis can be found neither in language nor in metalanguage. The solutions are always local, internal to the work; they are only useful once. At the same time, the establishment of local solutions itself remains fairly stable; it "creates a picture," as you have said, but only after redefining the encyclopedia itself.

MS Once again, there was a time when any philosopher worthy of the name was a dabbler in everything. The entire encyclopedia of knowledge of their times is found in the works of Plato, Aristotle, Saint Thomas, Descartes, Leibniz, Pascal, Hegel, Auguste Comte . . . and even, more secretly, in the works of Bergson. Kant wrote on arithmetic, geometry, astronomy, geography (he even read H. B. de Saussure's accounts of the first alpine expeditions), anthropology, history, theology. Do you call that dabbling in everything? Philosophy relies on a totalization of knowledge; he who practices it must do his fieldwork, must travel everywhere. At the very least it's like the labors of Hercules.

So, it's true that I assigned myself the task of working in this way, in every province of the encyclopedia. But today these areas are not systematic, or at least for my work I did not follow the usual order. Or, better yet, the present order seems like a chaos, in which a kind of rationality must be sought. This is the source of the seeming difficulty of my texts. Nonetheless, my books gradually sketch out the map of these provinces, including their historical moments. Indeed, one of the exciting problems of our era consists of rediscovering the chaotic nature of knowledge. I have even tried my hand at this, in the past.

In the course of this journey, which has often seemed endless, I have gradually come up with a theory of relations. This is why I worked on Leibniz—to my knowledge, he's the first philosopher of communication, in the area of the communication of substances, not relations. This is also why I chose Hermes as my patronymic. On the other hand, the sciences advance in proportion to how much they replace a given problem with the relations that make that problem possible.

BL It's impossible to simply ask, "What is Serres's ethic? what are his politics, his metaphysics?"

MS "Where are you?" "What place are you talking about?" I don't know, since Hermes is continually moving on. Rather, ask him, "What roadmap are you in the process of drawing up, what networks are you weaving together?" No single word, neither substantive nor verb, no domain or specialty alone characterizes, at least for the moment, the nature of my work. I only describe relationships. For the moment, let's be content with saying it's "a general theory of relations." Or "a philosophy of prepositions."

As for my ethic, I trust we will have the opportunity to speak of it another time. I don't want to die without having written it. The same for my politics.

BL All of this is very enlightening, at least for me, but today I'd like us to address the greatest difficulty encountered in reading your works—the one that makes you incomprehensible not for the technical reasons we've discussed up till now, but for a fundamental reason: your very conception of philosophy, of the era in which your philosophy takes place, and which seems to me to be defined by the phrase "the end of the critical parenthesis." For this I am going to ask you questions that you will not like, in order to outline, at first negatively and then positively, the philosophical era in which you situate yourself.

Far from Philosophies of Knowledge

BL   To begin with, you are not interested in what we might call the philoso-phy of knowledge?

MS   No, not at all. With my first Hermes book I wrote a text (which we have talked about) in which I took leave of epistemology, which is merely redundant commentary when compared to scientific results.

The place of commentary, of criticism, of judgment, of norms, even of foundations, is less plausible or interesting than the place of the thing judged or criticized. This is the reason for the useless-ness of the reflexive loop. The repetitive always contains less infor-mation; this diminishes with every copy. Science is founded on itself and, therefore, has no need of external philosophy; it con-tains its own endo-epistemology, if I may use this term. So, does the philosophy of science simply provide publicity for scientism?

BL   And, yet, doesn't it always asks the question that you never address—that of rationality?

MS   It doesn't ask the question; it considers the question as re-solved, no doubt since the Age of Enlightenment. Epistemology was born just after that era; there was no epistemology in the classical era, when, as you may have noticed, philosophers them-selves invented the sciences. So, this discipline marks the fact that the philosopher comes after the invention.

Epistemology implies that rationality exists only in the sciences, nowhere else. This is neither rationalism nor a valid and faithful description of rationality, but simply a hijacking, or what I would call publicity.

For reason and excellence can be found in many domains be-sides canonical science. Inversely, one can find in the latter as many myths as in old wives' tales. The best contemporary myth is the idea of a science purged of all myths. Again inversely, there is reason in mythologies, in religions—domains to which popular opinion today relegates only the irrational. In a certain way reason is, of all things in the world, the most equally distributed. No domain can have a monopoly on reason, except via abuse. In this regard each region is a mixed body.

BL Yes, but nonetheless your position is not in the least irrationalist, is it?

MS Not at all. I am a rationalist, in most of my actions and thoughts—like everyone! But I am not a rationalist if reason is defined as an ingredient only found in science. This restrictive definition is not reasonable. It's better to generalize it. Yes, I am a rationalist; how could I claim otherwise without losing reason? But this rationalism also applies to domains beyond science. In this regard the philosophies of the seventeenth century seem to me more reasonable than those of the following century, which marked the beginning of the exclusivity we're talking about.

For the rest, I belong to a generation formed entirely by the sciences, without having been constrained by the scientism of my predecessors. In other words, for us science was not a struggle, much less a Holy War. But I belong also and especially to the generation that saw science's coming to power, and also the advent of its ethical problems.

So, with regard to science, we practice a peaceful esteem and a certain unresentful agnosticism. For us it is neither absolute good nor absolute evil, neither total reason nor the forgetting of the human being, neither the Devil nor God, as preceding generations seemed to say. Science remains a means—no more, no less— but a system of means that has taken on so much social weight and importance that it is the only historical project remaining in the West. So, yes, indeed, philosophical problems begin to emerge.

BL Your point of departure always remains science, especially mathematics. You always strive to imitate the style and processes of the sciences. It's from them that you continue to borrow your metalanguage. But to give an idea of the abyss between the ideas that interest you and those that occupy 99 percent of the philosophy of contemporary science, both in France and in the United States—have you never been interested in the demarcation between what is truly science and what is truly not?

MS No. The history of the sciences shows (if history shows anything) that this border fluctuates continually, from one extremity of the heavens to the other. Who can't give a thousand examples of material that was not part of the sciences a little while ago and that suddenly became included in them—note the excellent theory of percolation—and as many examples of the reverse? Some very eminent mathematicians mocked me quite cruelly when I began to talk about chaos, more than fifteen years ago; now, with great efforts, they have managed to recapture the ball and run with it. The following is almost axiomatic: pay extra attention when it's said that something is "not science" (or, respectively, "not philosophy")—it could become it overnight. Inversely, how quickly canonized things become passé—tomorrow certain social sciences will be spoken of only with laughter.

To devote oneself to distinguishing such a demarcation requires quasi-divine efforts, like being able to part the waters of the Red Sea with a rod so the Hebrews can escape from Egypt. As for the wearing away of solid metaphors and the suppleness of fluids, don't imagine that the sciences and other bodies of knowledge are distributed like continents, surrounded by watery abysses. Not at all. They are more like the oceans—who can say exactly where the border between the Indian Ocean and the Pacific Ocean lies? Land masses are separated, but waters mix together; thus we have the clear and the obscure.

BL So, if rationalism's reason is to demonstrate precisely what is scientific and what is not—what is rational and what is not—then your reason is quite different.

MS Such an enterprise quickly turns into nonsensical work, whose outcome can only be comical. Auguste Comte, Kant, Hegel, and others tried to sketch out such lines of demarcation, but invention almost immediately canceled these out, or else they were ridiculed. We can count more planets than the number foreseen and fixed by Hegel in his famous thesis; topological space thumbs its nose at Kant's aesthetic (which is nonetheless transcendental), and astrophysics flattens positivist interdicts, if I may say so. To whom can we adhere? Time shakes up this kind of division, including those supposedly made by hardheaded reason. Don't forget the Marxists' prohibitions concerning the calculation of probabilities, indeterminism in physics, and bourgeois biology.

BL Let's move along now to philosophies of language. You understand, I am trying to have an overview of the philosophies that you have avoided but that probably were formative for your readers.

MS I'm very wary of this exercise you keep proposing, which consists of positioning me, so to speak, in a collectivity that you know better than I. Should I dare to admit it? When a person writes, he reads very little; there is not a lot of time. If one read everything, one would never write. Inversely, writing devours life, because it requires a crushing and monastic schedule. So, I have become fairly ignorant, especially in philosophy (which is what I secretly hoped for). So, what you are asking of me is nearly impossible—to trace my path in relationship to works that I only know by hearsay, or in relation to points that I only see fuzzily.

As for clarifying language—its use illuminates it as much as does analysis. What I mean is, to this end, exercising style is as valuable as grammatical surveillance. But don't mistake me—the philosophies that recommend this analysis and participate in it have considerable critical utility, because they avoid saying a lot of stupid things. I respect them; I recommend them to my students; I have even practiced them. As I told you, I was the first person in France to give courses in mathematical logic. But there again I find a demanding relationship between the enormous amount of energy required and the fairly weak results obtained. There's considerable expenditure and maximum work, in exchange for not much advancement. Didn't Wittgenstein himself say so?

And, I confess again—I prefer to move forward, even quickly, at the risk of falling, skipping over a few weak points. (Who doesn't do likewise, at some time, even among the most careful?) I prefer invention accompanied by the danger of error to rigorous verification, which is paralleled by the risk of immobility—in philosophy as in life, in life as in the sciences.

Let me refer you to a chapter in my book *Le Tiers-Instruit,* entitled "The Stylist and the Grammarian," in which I try to explain myself on the very matter of your question. In this text, which is arranged more in the form of a play than in that of a dialogue, the grammarian, who appears in several guises, represents the logician of the school you are talking about and is writing a grammar of objects. The stylist, on the other hand, wears the colors of what could be called a French-language school. But I want to remind you especially of my undertaking in *Les Cinq sens* [The Five Senses]. Pages 118–24 address your question even better. The project of this book dates from an immense flash of insight, which I will describe.

When I was young I laughed a lot when I read Merleau-Ponty's *Phenomenology of Perception.* He opens it with these words: "At the outset of the study of perception, we find *in language the notion of sensation....* " Isn't this an exemplary introduction? A collection of examples in the same vein, so austere and meager, inspire the descriptions that follow. From his window the author sees some tree, always in bloom; he huddles over his desk; now and again a red blotch appears—it's a quote. What you can decipher in this book is a nice ethnology of city dwellers, who are hypertechnicalized, intellectualized, chained to their library chairs, and tragically stripped of any tangible experience. Lots of phenomenology and no sensation—everything via language.

This same laughter bursts from me when I dip into a more recent work, J. Vuillemin's *La Logique et le monde sensible,* which begins by copying the axioms of the structure of order, like an elementary algebra text. Here in a nutshell are two opposing schools, the analytic and the continental, in which the return to things themselves halts at the same barrier—the logical.

I took great pleasure in leaping over this barrier. In so doing, without realizing it, I produced a pedagogical work, and elementary schoolteachers themselves have asked me to intervene in their work—what a reward . . .

All around us language replaces experience. The sign, so soft, substitutes itself for the thing, which is hard. I cannot think of this substitution as an equivalence. It is more of an abuse and a violence. The sound of a coin is not worth the coin; the smell of cooking does not fill the hungry stomach; publicity is not the equivalent of quality; the tongue that talks annuls the tongue that tastes or the one that receives and gives a kiss. My book *Les Cinq sens* cries out at the empire of signs.

But, to conclude, I request your indulgence in not asking me to judge. It's better to tell about what one has discovered than to criticize erroneously.

BL So, that eliminates the philosophy of sciences for us.

Far from a Judgmental Philosophy

MS I beseech you—don't say "eliminates"! I consider exclusion as history and mankind's worst action. No, let us not eliminate; on the contrary, let us include. I advise working on analytic philosophy and the movements associated with it, which are precious and formative. This is an excellent school, perhaps the best. What more can I say? I said it before about the history of philosophy, about demonstration, even about knowledge in general—they are good for training, for school, for teaching.

But the goal of school is to finish school; at a certain age it's appropriate to leave. One must actually become a farmer, after having learned the trade in agricultural school. At the end of training comes adulthood; the end, or the goal, of instruction is invention.

BL   Let's talk now about "philosophies of suspicion."

MS To press home my plea to dispense with judging, let me say a word about the philosophies that, seen from afar, made me run in the opposite direction—although they occupied my contemporaries, fascinating them for a long time. These are the philosophies Paul Ricoeur classified in the order or class of "suspicion."

I was turned off for two reasons. For one, these philosophies took up a position like spying, like looking over the shoulder of someone with something to hide. This position immediately invokes a third person, who in turn looks over the shoulder of the second, who now is also under suspicion, and so on, ad infinitum. This argument, a renewed version of the *third man,* opens up a vista of ongoing cunningness, like a succession of policemen and felons. As a result, philosophy becomes like a police state; in fact, every police force requires another police force to police it. When a policing body is looking over a person's shoulder, assessing his heart and innermost workings, are we to suppose that this policing body has neither a shoulder of its own, nor heart, nor innermost workings? This launches us into a "detective" logic. And the best detective is the one who is never interrogated, who places himself in a position beyond suspicion.

The critic's ultimate goal is to escape all possible criticism, to be beyond criticism. He looks over everyone else's shoulder and persuades everyone that he has no shoulder. That he has no heart. He asks all the questions so that none can be asked of him. In other words, the best policeman is the most intelligent felon. Critical philosophy ends with Inspector Dupin, who is invulnerable to it.

Better yet, what would you call the only person who could be imagined as looking over everyone's shoulder, without having a shoulder of his own? God. So, beware of philosophies that put he who practices them in the august position of always being right, of always being the wisest, the most intelligent, and the strongest. These philosophies always and eternally come down to strategies of war.

You wanted to talk about an ethic. Mine forbids me from playing that particular game. I willingly admit, before I begin, that I am not always right. This irenicism is the fundamental condition of intellectual honesty.

BL Yes, this is a trademark of your work, and we will talk more about it later: you are positive, not critical. One might even use the word positivist, if it weren't already taken. We will return to the reasons why you are not a philosopher of suspicion in an intellectual world that is entirely suspicious, why you are so naive, if I may say so.

MS As soon as philosophy enters academia, or develops exclusively there, this critical philosophy is born.

So, once again, why turn away from it? Because I don't like to scavenge. As I just said, I hate the idea of sneaking in without paying, as I hate all forms of cheating. It's not for nothing that I wrote a book about *The Parasite*, an animal who lives off another without the other even suspecting it. Here is the first commandment of the art of inventing: "Would you like to discover something new? Then stop cheating." Second, I don't like to look back; I prefer to advance.

And do we really know how to look back? Why is it done so badly? Because criticism, which likes to discern the "conditions of possibility" of a given process, usually confuses "necessary conditions" with "sufficient conditions." The necessary conditions for us to drink together today are global—a particular soil and grape vine, this generous and rare sun, geographic and human locality, our parents who gave us birth, time, which formed us—these are all necessary conditions, obvious and ordinary, which don't in any way explain what might be truly interesting: that you and I are saying what we are saying here and now. For that we would need to seek sufficient conditions.

But critics seek conditions that are global, general—all necessary, but which come down to mother, father, history, and economics—conditions necessary for everything and anything, always easy to find, since they are commonplace, but never useful. What does it really mean to me that this or that person had (like everyone, like you and me, perhaps) a cruel or a kind father and a gentle or abusive mother, that he ate black bread or white bread, under a monarchy or in a tyrannical democracy—in order to explain his writing a certain opera or a certain treatise on astronomy? Only sufficient conditions can get us out of this rut, but they will never come from our own efforts, never through any finite human power. Who has ever attained the sufficient conditions for one of Couperin's motets? So, here is another instance of wasted effort; the search for necessary conditions remains at the level of triviality—why undertake it? And sufficient conditions, for the moment, remain inaccessible. Such backward glances are bad.

Thus, criticism finds itself continually blocked between the trivial and the strongly inaccessible.

BL So, the "transcendental of relations" that we talked about before is totally different from conditions of possibility? You have never been interested in a project like Kant's, to organize, to verify foundations?

MS If foundations of this kind were really accessible, it would be known.

BL So, the philosophy of all possible relations is neither a foundation nor a condition of possibility?

MS It's true that in Latin, *conditio* also means the action of founding. One does not found a movement; a vortex or a curtain of flames is not like a piece of solid architecture.

BL What else estranges you from critical thought?

MS What bothers me in the practice of critical thought, I must say, is a characteristic that concerns the professional code of ethics of the work. It allows you to save an enormous amount of labor—for example, you can put in parentheses or cast doubt on the sciences without entering into their detail, in order to seek conditions or foundations—what a savings! A nice argument in favor of laziness, ignorance, or even cheating. By comparison, the philosophers of science are less deceitful; they go right to the source—right to the coal mine. I have a lot of respect for those who actually go to the mine, who take the trouble to go and see things on-site, who stay there, who take the tools in their hands, who have callouses on their palms and coal dust on their faces. Criticism has white hands. For a long time it has been described, rightly, as always at its ease.

It's better to do than to judge, to produce than to evaluate. Or, rather, it's in mining coal that one learns if it is gray or black. It's better to create than to criticize, to invent than to classify copies.

BL So, criticism—the exercise of criticism—repels you morally?

MS We'll talk later of the era of judging that philosophy has been in for a long time. New things are extraordinarily difficult to invent. If philosophy is worth an hour's work, it's in order to discover these things—or, better yet, to invent them—rather than to evaluate what is already done. Playing is better than blowing the referee's whistle. The philosophies you're talking about always place themselves on the side of judgment; thus they make decisions about the truth and clarity of a proposition, about its rationality, its modernity, about its faithfulness to existence. In this, they are academic: they classify and exclude, recognize and note. But it seems to me that the judge's real work or respect for the law lies elsewhere, as I will describe in a moment.

Philosophy aspires to give birth to a world both speculatively and in the domains of politics and professional ethics, rather than to crouch in an impregnable position from which it would have the right (inherited from I know not whom) to approve or condemn the modernity, rationality, or clarity of all discourses.

But this is not the main point, since, in fact, I am engaging here in criticism (*unjustly,* according to my own precepts) of criticism. If you are interested in law, as I am, you must see that our tradition—from the pre-Socratics to Hegel, by way of Plato, Aristotle, Spinoza, and Kant—seeks to discover an interesting and precise position from which one can see both law and science, scientific laws and juridical laws, these two kinds of reason. But this position is not one of criticism, since it necessarily lies outside of the law: it is a productive one. I sometimes wonder if it isn't a striking characteristic of Western philosophies. The crucial questions of our day still come from this place. It's not a matter of sitting in the judgment seat but, rather, of inventing a new set of laws.

The great problems of our era, since the dawn of Hiroshima, have to do with the whole set of relationships between the law and science. We must reinvent the place of these relations; we must therefore produce a new philosophy, so that lawyers can invent a new system of laws, and perhaps scientists a new science. As a result, this critical era no longer consists of giving philosophy the right to judge everything—a regal position from which it makes rulings right and left on everything—but the responsibility to *create*, to *invent*, to produce what will foster production, to invent or express a system of laws, to understand and apply a science.

BL So, your rejection of judgmental philosophy is not a rejection of a philosophy of law?

MS Of course not. Quite the contrary.

BL What appears unproductive to you in all these movements is not their ideas but their tendencies. They do not seem capable of artisanry?

MS They are not artistic in the Greek sense of the word, neither poetic nor productive. Don't all these tendencies seem to you like holdovers, end points, with neither dynamism nor capacity to take off again?

Far from Copernican Revolutions

BL But the rest of us, your readers, have been formed by these very holdovers, these very ends of the line. We believe that there have been definitive and decisive revolutions—absolutely radical, Copernican revolutions. In the sciences, this is the epistemological schism so dear to the followers of Bachelard. It's real—at least it was real—in politics, and it's real in the history of philosophy. These revolutions prevent us from communicating in a living fashion with the past, since the past is definitively abolished. We talked about this in our second session, but I would like to return to it now, because this belief in radical revolutions also has its positive side. It makes us modern and makes us incapable, I believe, of reading your work. But you are not critical even in your criticism of science.

MS I understand what you are trying to say. Do you know that this is a very old custom, our truly Western way of thinking, which cleaves time at revolutions? We live and think in a civilization *equipped with "antiquity"*—haven't you ever noticed how strange this must appear, from the outside? At a particular moment everything stops, and we start counting over again from zero and assign negative numbers to the preceding era. The Chinese don't compute time this way, nor do the Hindus. We think and live history by the kinds of ruptures you're talking about.

The same schema applies to science. Its prehistory—the era before it existed—is like an archaism that will henceforth remain buried, preceding the era when suddenly it arrives. How many philosophers use this effect to advantage? Before the Greeks no one thought; finally came the Greek miracle, which invented everything—science and philosophy. Or, better yet, there are those who divide everything into "before me, and then after my works." Descartes, Kant, and others proceed in this manner, as did Galileo, Lavoisier, and Pasteur in science. If we relativize this self-promoting mania, and if we now and again cast a different look at our scientific and technical exploits, as I do in the beginning of my book *Statues,* does the accident of the *Challenger* rocket strangely resemble the sacrifices to Baal, in Carthage? Indeed, a certain number of contemporary actions, behaviors, or thoughts repeat, almost without change, extremely archaic modes of thought or behavior. We are ancient in most of our actions and thoughts. This history by schisms or revolutions, which is more repetitive than any other, creates a screen that is so opaque and dark that we don't even see our veritable archaisms.

BL   Yes, but this is what the reader has a hard time putting up with!

MS Admittedly, it is hard for our narcissism to have our human sacrifices suddenly thrown in our faces.

BL For a simple reason—to be modern is precisely to accept that the Challenger *has nothing to do with Baal, because the Carthaginians were religious and we no longer are, because they were ineffectual whereas we are very effective, and so on.*

MS I talk about this at great length.

BL You do, in fact. But no one believes you because of this formidable difficulty that we are trying to explore here. You may make your point ten times, a hundred times, but no one believes you because the revolutions

that have made us modern have in fact made these past states incommensu-
rable. It's for this reason that we think of ourselves in a totally different
way than did the Carthaginians, except when we try to engage in exoticism.
I'm not repeating the question of time here, which we have already ad-
dressed; I am asking you a different, totally new question.

MS I understand, and I'm replying, in fact, on a different terrain.
The regime of revolutions is no doubt only *apparent*. What if,
behind them or beneath these schisms, flowed (or percolated)
slow and viscous fluxes? Do you recall the geological theory of
plate tectonics? Intermittent earthquakes result in sudden breaks
not far from known faults, like the San Andreas fault in California.
But underneath, continuous and extraordinarily slow movements
explain these sudden breaks where the quakes occur. And even
further below these continuous movements that pull, tranquilly
but inexorably, is a core of heat that maintains or propels the
moving crust. And what is the inner sun of these mechanisms?
Our old hot planet, which is cooling. Earth is that very sun.

Are the breaks in history similarly brought about from below
by an extraordinarily slow movement that puts us in communication with the past, but at immense depths? The surface gives the
impression of totally discontinuous ruptures, earthquakes—in this
case, quakes of history or of mobs, sometimes—whose brief violence destroys cities and remodels landscapes but which, at a very
deep level, continue an extraordinarily regular movement, barely
perceptible, on an entirely different scale of time.

May I say that in this we can glimpse the history of religions, for
example, which forms the lowest plate—the deepest, the most
buried, almost invisible, and surely the slowest moving. But what I
would like to catch a glimpse of, beyond that, and deeper yet, is
the furnace-like interior, so hidden, that blindly moves us.

For an Anthropology of the Sciences

BL All these points are difficult to understand. First of all because of the
structure of time, about which we have spoken in detail, but also because
our modern definitions make us consider Baal as a social phenomenon,
whereas the Challenger *rocket is a technical object.*

MS But also a social object. If not, would it be called *Challenger*? I'm sure you know that *challenge* is a transcription of the English pronunciation of the old French word *calomnie,* "calumny."

Just as the Romans built the Pont du Gard less for the purpose of transporting water by aqueduct than for the purpose of demonstrating their power to the local population, which was fascinated by this work of art, or in order to occupy the armies, which otherwise would have become restless and dangerous; likewise, don't you think that the Western nations explore space in order to demonstrate their power to the rest of the world, rather than for any useful reason?

BL Yes, but this distinction between orders of things organizes our way of representing not only modern science but also modern society. Some things belong in the domain of collective society, of culture, and some belong in the domain of nature. This is what usually organizes the critique of science, as when we say, "Science denatures; science is cold." The paradox is that you make a forceful critique of science, but you don't use the weapons of criticism, because you don't believe that science is cold; you find it as hot as Baal.

MS Do you think science would advance, inventively, without the intense heat of the spirit or of fire? Have we reached out and touched the motor that drives it? If so, we would feel that it burns, like a hellfire.

BL But you're performing a double operation there, which is doubly surprising. Ever since science came into existence we have heard three hundred years' of whining against it and its spread, its coldness, its abstract spirit—but you attribute neither these qualities nor these faults to it. You find it scarcely different from anything else. You leap over our revolutions and our epistemological breaks.

MS Or, rather, I dig underneath them, to discover (in the etymological sense) the system of slower-moving, hotter geological plates.

BL Science is at the same level as culture; it is as interesting, as dangerous; it has exactly the same qualities.

MS A car travels through space, which is an aspect of nature; it participates in a competition of egos on behalf of its owner, which is an aspect of culture, admittedly. When you put together these two vehicles (that really are one, of course), they allow us in our leisure time—solemnly, on holidays—to assuage our unslakable thirst for human sacrifice to the gods, whom we think we have forgotten. Our god is the machine, the technical object, which stresses our mastery of our surroundings, which regulates certain group relations or certain viscous psychological relations, but which suddenly plummets, like a lead weight, into the depths of a formidable anthropology. Take this adjective *formidable* in its classical sense, meaning "terrifying"; we scarcely dare to look in the direction of this sun. You see how we pass without a break from science—in this case thermodynamics and materials resistance—to technology, and from there to sociology, then to the history of religion, which, as I just said, comes close to the fiery core.

Yes, the sciences are indeed cultural formations, among others, and I don't need to tell you that in general our tools—for example, the *Challenger*—are simultaneously objects of this world and objects of society. Every technology transforms our rapport with things (the rocket takes off for the stratosphere) and, at the same time, our relations among ourselves (the rocket ensures publicity for the nations that launch it). Certain instruments, certain theories, lean more in one direction, others in another, but all show both aspects as well.

BL But it's extremely difficult to understand this "as well." There are at least two types of critique of science. First there is that of the epistemologists, who criticize it because it is not rational enough. Once science is in their hands, they say, it will be even more rational—finally purged of all traces of the collective. On the other hand, there are critiques of science that attribute to it what you deny in it: the capacity to be cold and rational.

MS Rationally pure.

BL This is the reason for the importance of the expression "anthropology of science," which you use in your book Statues. *In your writing—in Rome, for example—in your fifteen origins of geometry, there is a whole mythology of science's anthropological actions—purifying, washing—that plunges the sciences once again into that very past they claim to have left behind forever.*

MS Yes, my book on Lucretius, for example, shows how the terms *atom* and *vacuum* are positioned halfway between the author's claims to rationality and physics, and his religious narratives, like the sacrifice of Iphigenia. Both words indicate a crisscrossing: the word *atom* belongs to the same family as *temple,* and the word *vide* [vacuum] indicates, by its Latin and Greek roots, the act of catharsis [see *Lucrèce* (165)].

BL But the main difficulty in interpreting your works comes from the fact that you don't approach science from the point of view of collective society. Science, in fact, is talking about things. *And this is why, on the other hand, you reproach sociology, literature, and politics for not being interested in* things, *for being what you call "a-cosmic."*

MS Why do the human or social sciences never talk about the world—as though groups were suspended in a vacuum? And why are the so-called hard sciences at an impasse where humanity is concerned? Their respective absences outline each other's presences. How can our main disciplines remain so hemiplegic?

It seems to me that one of philosophy's tasks is to teach these disciplines to walk with both feet, to use both hands. As you know, my book *Le Tiers-Instruit* calls left-handed people who have been forced to use the right hand "complete bodies" and praises those hybrids and mixtures that appall philosophies of purity. Isn't it more reasonable to use both hemispheres of the brain in unison?

BL But you are always tripping up your readers; you are always operating simultaneously on two opposing fronts. When they think they are reading about collective society, you bring them back to things, *and then, when they think they are reading about the sciences, you bring them back to society. They go from Baal to the* Challenger *and then from the* Challenger *to Baal!*

MS It's a magnificent paradox, which I savor. To walk on two feet appears to mean tripping everyone up. Is this a proof, then, that we always limp?

Yes, we live in the world; our collectivity inhabits it and tries to understand it. Philosophy resides at this junction, and our recognition of this place and of its future, habitable or not, quickly forces us to question the rapports between the law and science, which we just talked about. If not, the law and social sciences remain without a world—a-cosmic—and the natural sciences, without the law, become inhuman. Today we live and think at this crossroads.

BL No, not exactly. The sciences are not somehow more cosmic; they are more polemical, more collective, noisier, than many other areas of our lives—that's what you demonstrated to everyone in your texts on thanatocracy. Neither your definition of the collective nor your definition of science is a stable target. Neither one corresponds to what criticism (basically, your readers) imagines and expects, because yours is not a critique in the classical sense. Even if sometimes in your work you use a more classical theme to criticize science—for its absence of soul, for its ugliness, etc., a theme that is clearly antimodern, even undeniably rural—it's never the main theme. Your main argument is quite simply to not recognize science's totally different character . . .

MS Which is its nature. And thanks for the "rural"—I'm even rustic, if you will; I much prefer living in the country to the city.

Further, I'll mention in passing that I consider ecological ideologies to be the umpteenth instance of the city and city dwellers' trans-historical victory over the fields and the woods. In eliminating country folk, city dwellers have made open spaces into a desert, which is the source of a thousand tragedies.

Finally, and most important, my book *The Natural Contract* explicitly ridicules agrarian ontologies, which are dangerous, in order to substitute for "the land"—the patchwork fields of the bloody battles of our ancestors—the global Earth, the planet, which must be thought about, at new costs. Far from remaining buried in one locality, this book seeks the passage from the local to the global. This is the very book in which I find it, and I will stick with it hereafter.

But let's get back to the nature of the sciences . . .

BL And to the source of their pride. You do not acknowledge either their pride or their danger. This is something the reader finds difficult. This is what I meant by "Copernican revolution." As far as you are concerned, nothing irreversible has happened that makes us modern. I'm tempted to say that you are not modern in this sense.

Let's Not Keep Repeating the Gesture of the Copernican Revolution

MS Perhaps I am not, in fact, modern, in the sense that you give that term. But what difference does it make, basically, if I am this or that, described by an adjective? More, to the point, who is qualified to say so? What is the point of pinning it down? Only children and adolescents are preoccupied—intensely, passionately, madly, as their first formation—in being this or that, in order to be more attractive to others. Adults get busy and act and could care less what they are.

But let's move in the direction you suggest. It's my turn to ask a question. What if those who claim to be modern are, in fact, ancient? What if the modern are very rare? So-called modernity presumes that there was a revolution that changed a certain state of affairs, making way for a new era, right?

But this idea or maneuver—this gesture—has been repeated so often in our history that one wonders if Western thought has ever ceased starting over again, automatically, like a reflex, since its beginnings. At least since Adam and Eve were driven from the Garden of Eden—they had to start again from scratch. Then came the birth of the Messiah.... This way of being modern exactly defines our repeated (I would say archaic) habit. The famous preface to the *Critique of Pure Reason* marks out for each science an initial moment from which everything began, leaving in its wake a kind of antiquity. If being modern requires us to repeat this gesture, nothing is more ancient. When one repeats a gesture, is one modern? Conservative? Archaic?

BL So, you—you are modern, in this new sense? Even though you don't read the newspapers, you must have heard of postmodernism: it's a journalists' term that philosophers have taken seriously. It's an absurd theme, but it's nonetheless the chic, cultural era in which we find ourselves. We are no longer modern, they say, but postmodern. Postmodernism is disappointed rationalism, combining the effects of rationalism and disappointment, and, as for you, I would tend to say that you were never modern. But you yourself say to me, "I am the only one who is truly modern."

MS Perhaps. But you are putting me through the same ordeal. You're asking me to situate myself in relation to a debate that is unfamiliar to me. How could I reply without saying stupid things? When you're busy working, you couldn't care less about "situating" yourself. Either you situate yourself, which takes an incredible amount of time, given the astronomical number of bibliographic names to be included, or you work, which takes *all* your time, all your energy, your entire life. For this reason it is difficult to situate oneself.

BL   But I'm doing my job, and I'll keep at it! So, if I understand rightly, you are modern in the sense that you are the only one who does not repeat the maneuver of absolute, radical rupture, which cuts the past off behind us?

MS I have never claimed to do anything absolutely new, unheard of, never seen before; this would be to use the language of advertising. As for the novelty of someone's work, it can only be judged plausibly by the fourth or fifth generation after him. For example, we are just beginning to realize that Sartre's work was neither so new nor so politically committed as he claimed in his time—meaning the time of the atomic bomb, of the new sciences, of antibiotics, of the Pill, of the growth, parallel and vertical, of technical objects and the population.

And yet there is nothing more interesting, in a given domain, than introducing newness. To me, to discover seems the only act of intelligence. To discover [*trouver*] not in the intellectual sense, but in the sense of the medieval *trouvères,* the troubadours. It's much harder than we think to guard against accepted ideas, because often the ideas that seem the most modern, that suddenly mobilize a whole community—its media and its conversations—are agreed-upon ideas. In order for an idea to circulate it needs to be polished; it always takes years for it to acquire that smooth surface that enables it to circulate. This is why the ideas that circulate are usually astonishingly old. Thus, he who seeks newness remains alone.

BL   I think we are barking up the wrong tree—because for me "modern" does not mean new, modernist, modernizing. I understand it in its more philosophical sense. To be modern is to make the Copernican revolution twice, by making the division of the past from the present and by making the absolute division between the known world and the mind that knows it: this is the meaning that Kant gives to modernity in his preface. To state it in more anthropological terms, it means an absolute division between collective society and the real world—between Baal and the Challenger. *The fact of wanting to do new things . . .*

MS So, that's what being modern is?

BL Let's say it's the concept I have found that brings together all the difficulties of reading your work. To be modern is to make the absolute separation between the collectivity and things, a separation that estranges us absolutely from mythology, from the past, from other cultures—a separation that sets us apart. For example, the Greeks, and to an even greater degree the Carthaginians, are totally immersed in the collective. They can't distinguish between the world and representations of it, whereas we, as moderns, can.

MS We are no better at it than they were, when you come right down to it. We separate those concerned with the social sciences from those who make an impact on the world.

BL Yes, in fact, I believe that your anthropology of the sciences resolves this question. For you, being modern means not repeating Kant's work of purification. So, that means that you have never been modern in the sense that I propose; you have never had behind you a Copernican revolution that forever abolishes the past and sets us totally apart. Everything that you do is "in the midst."

MS All right.

BL The fact that you innovate, that you take so many risks, is a result of this position. So, you are not antimodern, archaicizing (at least it's not your principal theme); you are obviously not postmodern; you are not modern in the sense of modern criticism, which definitively separates nature and culture, past and present. I'm tempted to say that you are a-modern, or nonmodern, meaning that in retrospect you see (and we see, through your books) that we have never been modern, if we reread our past without all the Copernican and political revolutions—if we remove Kant, Marx, Bachelard. There is no more epistemological rupture.

MS Right.

Far from Exposure and Denunciation

BL So, now we arrive at the source of the single greatest difficulty for your readers who were trained by the "masters of suspicion." You said a while ago that you did not like the philosophers of suspicion or the philosophers of foundations, for reasons of professional ethics, for moral reasons.

MS Yes, I said so. I will add, for legalistic reasons. Why does philosophy, in every proceedings that it initiates, take the role of public prosecutor? The role of denouncer? Why, and by what right? The thought of a philosophy that uses police-type methods—to the point of trying to be cleverer than Inspector Dupin—and that criticizes in order to subpoena, like a public official, appalls me.

BL   But it is likewise for moral reasons, for reasons of professional ethics, that other philosophers don't like you—or, rather, that they ignore you. For them, philosophy's entire work, both intellectual and political, consists of exposing, of denouncing. If you remove the weapon of suspicion, the weapon of criticism, there is no further terrain for their intellectual work— for denouncing, for exposing, even for explication. For this reason you appear naive. Your work is not a critique; it's not an exposure; it's not even an explication—you often use the opposition between explication and implication. What is the normal work of a philosopher? He founds, he judges, he denounces, he exposes, he offers the critical repertoire that allows for subsequent action. You have never practiced any of this repertoire. But this is what makes modernity, what defines the task of the intellectual from the political point of view . . .

MS To accuse, to expose, to found, to shed light—on the contrary, the analysis of the *Challenger* explosion indeed casts a shadow on the landscape.

BL   Yes, because the Challenger *becomes as somber as Baal.*

MS Yes, my books *Rome* and *Statues* often praise the Roman or Egyptian gesture of burying, of concealing, of hiding, of placing something in the shadows in order to conserve it, as opposed to the Greek gesture of bringing things into the light. These works even praise implication—the folding of the pastry dough by the baker—more than explication. Here two types of knowledge stand face to face, but we only practice and esteem the second. Our culture plunges toward these two complementary roots, Greek and Latin, and not toward a single one, but we only privilege one of them. But to wrench something from the shadows often is to destroy it, while to place something in the shadows is often to protect it. We never calculate the cost of our methods; we believe they are free. Everything has its price, even clarity: it's paid for in shadows or destruction, sometimes.

We should invent a theory of obscure, confused, dark, nonevident knowledge—a theory of "adelo-knowledge." This lovely adjective, with feminine resonances, means something that is hidden and does not reveal itself. The Greek island of Delos was once called Adelos, the hidden one. If you have tried to approach it, you surely know that it is usually hidden in clouds and fog. Shadow accompanies light just as antimatter accompanies matter.

BL You make criticism obscure by implicating it in an archaism it thought itself rid of forever. What's more, you mix things (the most unpardonable crime in criticism); you mix the pole of objects and the pole of the collective. So, all this work of purification that defines criticism and defines the two hundred years of philosophy since Kant has never interested you. You have never believed in the modern world—in the modern philosophical task, in exposing, in denouncing—even though, for you, this means that you have been truly modern, this time in the sense of contemporary, current.

MS Because that kind of work really prevents one from understanding. I believe that the *Challenger* affair is seen best as I show it. This fleshes it out. This object, which we thought simply brought us into a relationship with the stars, also brings us into relationships among ourselves. It's at this point that it occupies its full reality. When we place society on one side and science on another, we no longer see anything.

A certain light, strong and focused, dazzles the eyes, whereas placing an object in light and shadow allows us to see it. Actually, we always see in this way, in the light and shadow of the real atmosphere. The pure light of the sun would burn our eyes, and we would die of cold in the darkness.

BL Yes, the essential activity of modernity consists of shedding light by exposing. The postmodernists have all the disadvantages; they are rationalist and disappointed. Whereas you, you have all the advantages; you are neither rationalist nor disappointed. But in order to see this advantage we must absolve you of an unpardonable crime: you mix together the Challenger *and Baal, whereas all the work of criticism has been in separating, in distinguishing what was collective in Baal and what was science and technology in the* Challenger. *This is why your anthropology of the sciences remains incomprehensible, in my opinion, even if we have overcome the difficulties of reading addressed thus far. You need to explain this passage, this sideways movement, this philosophical project that is different from criticism.*

Ju-piter: After the Dual Unveiling, Everything Remains to Be Done

MS Those distinctions are not separations that exist in reality.

On this subject there is an analysis of Jupiter's name in *Rome* [210–13, English ed.]. This is a proper name composed of two words, the first of which means *jour* (day) and the second of which means *père* (father). *Ju* in fact harks back to the Indo-European radical that evokes physical light and is found in the French word *jour*. *Piter* is only a slight variation on *pater* (father). So, *Jupiter* is equivalent to "light-father," or to "Our Father who art in Heaven." On the one hand, heavenly light and, on the other, the paternal relationship.

Let's first turn to physics, in order to study the light in the heavens. This hard science and the laws of electrostatics teach us, for example, that Jupiter does not hurl lightning bolts but that they are produced by electrical charges. Thus, the laws of nature are substituted for religion. Physics allows us to leave the religious sphere. This is what can be called the physicalist critique of mythology, carried out since the Age of Enlightenment, which is even named accordingly.

Afterward came the Age of Romanticism, the age of the heart— another instance of religion. Lamartine prays: "Holy Father, adored by my father, you who are only named on bended knee, you whose mighty and gentle name makes my mother bow her head. It's said that this brilliant sun is only a plaything of your power . . ." [translated from the Pléiade edition of *Oeuvres de Lamartine*, (314–15)]. Once the first name, Ju, has been sanitized, explained, made explicit, criticized—and thereby expelled—there remains the Père, Father. To put it another way, after the Age of Enlightenment and rationalist or physicalist explanation, what remains for religion is sentiment—the part that is not physical but human. *Jour*/light exits; *Père*/Father remains.

Let's turn now to those social sciences that explore paternal relations, family structures, and the emotions attached to parental relations. Once the "Piter," or *pater,* of religion has been sanitized, explained, made explicit, criticized—and thereby expelled—by the suspicious era of the social sciences, exit the Father.

Ju was clarified by the physical sciences and *Piter* by the social sciences. "Our Father" is known to us from now on; "who art in Heaven"—this place is even better known to us. Freud, Nietzsche, the anthropologists and psychoanalysts (not to mention the linguists), have explained the former to us; for the latter we have read Maxwell, Poincaré, or Einstein. Consequently, there is no more religion.

So, the death of God is well documented and dated. After the reign of the social sciences, religions find themselves in a worse state today than at the end of the eighteenth century, on the eve of the French Revolution, immediately following the victory of physical rationalism.

BL This is another way of describing the opposition between the Challenger *and Baal—on the one hand, the rationalists' criticism of the collective's influence on scientific reason and, on the other, social science's criticism of science's misplaced "naturalization."*

MS However, we still need to understand why *Ju* and *Piter* are associated or were placed and pronounced together. Why a hyphen (absent or traced between the two of them) reunites them, why a tie so powerful that it's like cement holds them together, why no one thinks of writing a comma between *Our Father* and *who art in Heaven.*

No matter what critique has been accomplished by the physical sciences on the side of light *(jour)* and the world, and no matter what critique has been done by the social sciences on the side of the *pater,* of social authority and the human heart—it still remains to be understood why we live with our father in the light of day. The fact remains that my father once walked hand in hand with me under the same sun under which I now walk with my grandchildren, and neither the social sciences nor the physical sciences take into account this coexistence of the social group and the world.

Here's some heavy evidence: human collectives survive under the light of the heavens; we are in the world together; ours is a reality both cold and warm, physical and carnal; we live in society under the light of day.

No scientific knowledge sheds light on this evidence or this mystery. I do not read any science in this absence of a hyphen between *Ju* and *Piter*. Religion returns through this absence. This is why philosophy still has a lot of work ahead of it.

BL And why everything is beginning. This is why you are not a postmodern, a disappointed rationalist.

MS Three problems presented themselves. Admittedly, in the beginning it was necessary to separate Ju (who art in Heaven—the physical sciences) from Piter (Father—the social sciences) and explain everything separately on both sides. Once these two problems are resolved, once the roads have been invented along which they successively resolve themselves—once the global network of the encyclopedia has been followed—Jupiter remains, in his entirety, which we have not yet grasped.

We have not yet understood the formidable alliance between the statue of Baal and the *Challenger* rocket—why a single object fashioned by our hands, the product of our relations and our ideas, concerns the world. Why are we there, arguing, making war, beneath the indifferent light of day? Why do we love one another under the laws of physical science? This absent link would be a good subject for philosophy.

BL And you have never stopped asking this question?

MS That's right. How is sociology situated in astronomy (the two sciences most distant from each other since the positivists' classification)? This is the question asked by all the texts in *Les Origines de la géométrie*. How are politics situated in physics? This is the great question of *The Natural Contract*. How are technology and physics situated in the anthropology of death? This is the question in *Statues*. How do you fit together parasitology, information theory, and the literature or ethnology of table manners? This is the question of *The Parasite*. How do you situate thermodynamics with genetics and both of them with the history of religion? This is the question addressed in my book on Zola. And how do you situate the symmetry/asymmetry of left and right, of orientation, of *sense* in the physical sense (direction) of the word, with *sense* in the human (very general, not just sexual) sense of the word? This is the question in *L'Hermaphrodite*. These are some of the questions explored in *Le Passage du Nord-Ouest* and that *Le Tiers-Instruit* recommends teaching.

In sum, I repeat: How do we live and think together beneath a light that warms our bodies and models our ideas, but which remains indifferent to their existence? We contemporary philosophers cannot ask this question while ignoring the sciences, which, in their very separation, converge to ask it, even to exacerbate its terms.

And when "the world" means purely and simply the planet Earth, we come back to the questions asked in *The Natural Contract:* when humanity is finally solidary and global in its political existence and in the exercise of science, it discovers that it inhabits a global Earth that is the concern of our global science, global technology, and our global and local behaviors. This is the reason for the necessary synthesis I spoke of a while ago.

Do you accuse me of mixing things together? I would have stayed in the analytical tradition if there were only those two problems—those that the sciences solve together, respectively. But there are three of them. Only the third one forces us to philosophize on the inextricable and transparent knot that ties Jupiter together: the shadowy cementing together of *Jour*/Light and *Père*/Father. This is the reason for my most recent texts and narratives on the bond in general—the texts that annoy you so much.

So, let's not add our voices to those of the headlines crying out for a renewal of religious sentiment. You can read similar themes in antiquity and a similar style in the daily news. Likewise, don't join them in saying that philosophy is finished, for every conceivable reason. Rather, it is just beginning. We have a tremendous opportunity.

BL So, I analyze your position rightly, in saying that it is nonmodern. If being "modern" is defined as the task that separates Ju *from* Piter—*which, as Kant said in his preface, is the only way to set metaphysics on the safe road as a science, and effectively to put God out of the picture in this affair . . .*

MS This is why I took the example of a god or of God—in other words, the most difficult or delicate example.

BL So, in the modern configuration, in this critical parenthesis that opens with Kant and closes now with you, we have the cosmic pole, given over in general to the exact sciences, and we have the pole of the collective, given over to the social sciences. We have God, who is out of the picture, banished. And, thanks to this configuration, we are going to have a dual exposure—by attacking the false powers of obscurantism, thanks to the discoveries of science, and by attacking the false power of science, thanks to the discoveries of the social sciences . . .

MS Since we have performed two unveilings, we believe we are at the end—at the maximal amount of light on the side of physical laws, and at the utmost clarity on the side of suspicion. But these two distinctions, side by side, make a nice effect of obscurity.

BL And there is no agreement, except in the criticism of religion, twice over, both from the point of view of the first unveiling (that of the eighteenth century of the Aufklärung) and a second time from the point of view of the social sciences (thanks to the second unveiling, the alienation of the nineteenth century).

MS That's it. And, satisfied intellectually, we don't see that religion remains intact, in the absence of the hyphen. Springing up from that spot, it suddenly inundates everything else. An inundation so deep today that we can no longer see its source.

BL But at the very moment when we believe we are so clever, so terribly modern, this is when we become postmodern, because suddenly the postmodernists have the impression that there's nothing more to do; they are sad, when actually they have not even begun!

MS The last third of the work seems to me the most important. As a result, the expression "anthropology of the sciences" is not so badly chosen, since it straddles what Jupiter's name bridges: anthropology for the affairs of the father and physical sciences for the laws of light.

BL We were talking about clarifications, and we stumble on a double clarity—to illuminate the clarity of a link. And yet it is for this very reason that you are called obscure, because this link is hidden by the dual exposure, which for two hundred years has been the definition of clarity, clarification, illumination—the Age of Enlightenment.

MS Except it must be said that here "enlightenment" reveals a chiaroscuro—a light and dark. But darkness is not necessarily a negative quality. No, here we're not talking about the light of a platonist sun, nor that of the Aufklärung—so purely physical that it blinds us toward the social sciences—nor is it a question of distinguishing, since we are trying to understand the famous link. Rather, we are talking about a fairly soft and filtered light that allows us better to see things in relief, through the effects of contrast produced by rays and shadows that melt together, that are mixed, nuanced.

This is the way we see ordinarily, really, daily—with our bodily eyes, in our concrete surroundings. On the moon and on planets without atmosphere, which lack this tranquil or turbulent air in which the sun's rays are lost and mixed, giving us true vision and a temperate existence, the sun's light geometrically cuts the night's shadows. On one side too much fire and dazzlement prevent vision and life; on the other are death and blindness through cold and darkness. So, the clear and distinct knowledge of analysis has its place, on the moon, where the rational and the irrational are clearly separated—minus two hundred degrees on the one side, more than two hundred degrees on the other. We have known for a long time why philosophers should not "live on the moon": it's too dangerous.

The flowing air responsible for mingling carries the links in question. In philosophical parlance, these gusts of wind used to be called the spirit.

Closing the Critical Parenthesis

BL We can now return positively to what we had started by defining negatively. All the philosophies we touched upon were of no interest to you, to the extent that they did not make this link comprehensible. This is why I kept returning to criticism and why you are interested in the eighteenth century, in the seventeenth century, in the Greeks and the Romans—in precisely all the centuries and all the philosophers prior to when they considered it their duty to make this distinction.

MS In fact, Lucretius immerses atomic physics in an environment that begins with the sacrifice of Iphigenia and ends with the plague of Athens. In general, my books immerse technology in anthropology and environmental physics or climatology in politics and law, and also the reverse. More generally, the immersion itself is fascinating—the flowing milieu of this immersion.

BL Kantianism doesn't interest you for all the reasons you gave about foundations but also for the fundamental reason that it purifies these two extremes—the known object, the knowing subject. But in dialectics don't dialecticians also claim to make a synthesis between the object and the subject—don't they claim to discover this fusion, this coproduction? Don't they also claim to escape from dualism, to immerse collective society and nature in the same history that is that of salvation?

MS Dialectics recites a logic so impoverished that anything and everything can be drawn from it. In it you have only to set up a contradiction, and you will always be right. *Ex falso sequitur quodlibet*—From the false comes anything. Contradiction enables you to deduce anything from anything. Ever since the invention of classical formal logic we have known that it's possible to deduce anything, true or false, from contradiction, from the pairing of true and false, and that this deduction is valid. This is the source of the dialectic ensemble of constructions, of deductions—each more valid than the last, but totally without interest. Even in their logical trappings war or polemics remains sterile.

BL But let's take the example of Bergson. I'm choosing philosophers who are not well liked, to see if our preceding discussion will allow us to rightly test the history of philosophy and thereby remove the main difficulty of reading your works.

MS Thanks for bringing him into the discussion. Bergson addressed some appropriate problems at the appropriate time, often way ahead of his time.

BL Nonetheless, there is in Bergson a conception of reification, of geometrization, which is absolutely contrary to your anthropology of the sciences, right?

MS Let's make a distinction between two things—what he says and how he does it. His critical analysis of the solid metaphor is literally sublime.

BL So, it's his philosophical style rather than his results that interest you.

MS Yes.

BL Are there other philosophers, who, like you, would not be modern, as I have defined it?

MS Always the same ordeal, which brings me back to my estrangement from contemporary things.

BL It's astonishing to see that there aren't that many resources for being nonmodern. Because you have to look elsewhere; you have to go back to at least before the eighteenth century, you have to accept metaphysics, rediscover ontology; you have to accept doing precisely what one has been taught . . .

MS . . . not to do.

BL Not to do?

MS To mix what's analyzed.

BL But, as a result, you deprive us of the weapon that seems the most important in criticism—that is, exposure, denunciation. This is the essential problem. You don't give us the means to expose the position of the other . . .

MS To mix and combine in the places in which you would analyze—isn't this henceforth a good methodology? The example of Jupiter demonstrates it fairly well. I don't challenge the two efforts to clarify the two sides—quite the opposite. But once you have done this you are no further along, because you haven't understood the link that unites them.

BL You haven't understood it either if you make them into a contradiction.

MS Even less so. How can it be understood? Religion has a long road ahead of it, since it still takes on this ancient problem we were talking about. Religion still shoulders this burden. And we philosophers should seek it there, to clarify it even more.

BL Religion used to carry it.

MS It used to carry it; it still carries it.

BL It carries it almost without realizing it, since religion itself is now rationalized to its core.

MS Or, rather, irrationalized. Religion ceased to appear rational at the end of the eighteenth and beginning of the nineteenth centuries, between Rousseau and Romanticism.

BL In both cases it accepted the takeover of the sciences. Theology doesn't come to our rescue directly. It is itself too scientistic.

MS Remember the nineteenth-century explanations of the origin of religions: it was always a matter of attributing divinity to natural forces—wind, rain, or volcanoes. The ancestors we invented for ourselves were always presumed to be terrorized by storms and floods. Being physical in origin, religion was charged with describing the origins of physics.

On the other side of the coin, today we prefer anthropological origins—violence, murder, royal sacrifice. In the first case there is no father; in the second he never sees the light of day.

Either men are alone, confronted by nature, with neither group nor society, or they begin to live politically, and, then, no more world. The famous rupture between the natural state and the social state only projects the same schism into time—an imaginary and theoretical time or history. This rupture concerns theories of knowledge, of history, the history of religion and philosophy, not counting our concrete practices of teaching and of polluting the Earth.

BL It's not altogether true that the two explanatory projects remain in the same state that they were.

MS No, not entirely.

BL Because the scientific enterprise loses its realism, or at least its externality (which is nonetheless the goal of Kant's operation, and of others). I mean that the Challenger *is no longer outside society. And, on the other hand, the collective society of the social sciences loses its social aspect. A social aspect that is built with heaviness—with black holes, with the* Challenger—*is no longer the same social aspect; at any rate it's not the one studied by sociology. Thus, we lose two times: things-in-themselves and people-among-themselves. The word* myth *changes meaning completely. It's a little too ecumenical to say, "We'll keep the two extremes, the dual exposure, and now we'll move along to an analysis of the hyphen between them."*

MS You are right, that changes things completely—as in a chemical reaction. What is blue becomes violet, thus remaining somewhat blue, but edging toward red and, on the other side, edging toward green.

Speaking of all this, tell me, why do they say, "Humanity's great histories are over" or "We no longer live out great stories"?

BL Ah! So you do read the newspapers!

MS Well, occasionally one has to sit in the dentist's waiting room. But how can they say this, when we're on the point of writing new histories and stories, tremendous ones, and, meanwhile, a lot of other ones are still functioning?

BL This is typically postmodern, having exactly the same structure as this dual unveiling you explain.

MS Triple!

BL No, no, wait—precisely, for the postmoderns, there are only two. Without this they would not be postmodern. There is that of science and that of suspicion. As far as postmodernity is concerned, you are on the outside and woefully naive.

MS You are totally right. I don't question this naïveté in the least. Ever since my student days I have felt that I have remained naive, in comparison to my contemporaries. But thus I naively ask, how can the non-naive claim to have gone beyond scientific questions without ever having looked closely at them?

BL Yes, but over the last two hundred years philosophers have developed the critical resources that make your quest so difficult for your readers.

MS When you really do the indispensable work on one of the two sides and then on the other, you quickly realize that you can't do the one without being able to tie into the other at a certain point. There is some mythology in science and some science in mythology. What remains is to recount this immense history or legend, without fragmentation.

BL Unfortunately, this argument doesn't work, because people still see this abysslike dichotomy where you, on the other hand, see a fundamental hyphen—the source of all your elucidations.

MS Yes—the dichotomy is there in people's heads. And in institutions, in the newspapers, in conventional exchanges—in "mainstream intellectual movements," as the saying goes. Everywhere. Except in the inventive, active sciences and in old wives' tales. Except at the extreme crest, narrow and rapid, and in the slowest base. Except at the summit of the mountain, which one attains after extreme efforts and a whole life of training. And among the old people in the thatched houses in the valley. Except at the peak and at the base. In the middle the usual exchange is surrounded by clouds, fog, and vapors.

BL The dichotomy is there in people's heads. It is in the definition of modernity, in the definition of criticism, even in our professional ethics. For an intellectual it is the very source of his own dignity, of his self-respect. When you present this argument you rob intellectuals of their respect.

MS But not of their work.

BL But of their work as it was defined by criticism. "What is left for us to do if we no longer denounce false representations with the help of the hard sciences or the social sciences?" Postmodernism is a journalistic invention that is not even worth talking about, and yet it is a symptom of the greatest difficulty. The fact that your readers are not modern in the sense in which you are is the source of all their other errors in reading your work. Everyone will object, "But the Challenger *is not Baal."*

MS It is, and it isn't. Furthermore, as a third position, we must hold both affirmations at once.

Kepler's Ellipse and Its Double Center

BL If you resolve the problem of modernism, then the problem of differences recurs. None of the differences is going to resume the position it had in relation to Kant's two poles. But there are differences, nonetheless. This is what you call "substitution" in Statues *and what you previously had called "translation." So, it seems to me that there is a double test—first you link Baal and the* Challenger, *then they have to exchange their properties in a symmetrical fashion. We are supposed to understand the Carthaginians' practice of human sacrifice by immersing ourselves in the* Challenger *event, but, inversely, we are supposed to understand what technology is through the Carthaginian religion.*

MS Yes, the reasoning is more or less symmetrical.

BL That's the first part of the test—first the link, then a double illumination. But next there are differences. The Carthaginians cry out, "These are cattle, not children"; we cry out, "It's the conquest of space that requires sacrifices; it's not the collective, the Moloch of the collective."

MS It's not so simple. We could construct a kind of dictionary that would allow us to translate, word by word, gesture by gesture, event by event, the scene at Cape Canaveral into the Carthaginian rite, and vice versa. The list is in *Statues* [13–34]: the respective cost of the operation, comparable for the two communities, the immense crowd of spectators, the specialists who prepare it and who are apart from the rest, the ignition, the state-of-the-art machinery in both cases, given the technology of the two eras, the organized or fascinated rehearsal of the event, the death of those enclosed in the two statues, whose size dominates the surrounding space, the denial you were just talking about—"No those aren't humans, but cattle," cry even the fathers of the incinerated children in Carthage; "No," we say, "it wasn't on purpose, it wasn't a sacrifice, but an accident," inevitable, even calculable, through probabilities.

The two columns list a series of substitutions between modernity and antiquity and also between the physical or technical and religion—in other words, from Ju- to Piter, effortlessly. The series of substitutions functions exactly like stitches, like mending a tear, like making a nice tight, overcast seam—*un surjet* (in mathematics, a surjection). Each term of the translation passes on a piece of thread, and at the end it may be said that we have followed the missing hyphens between the two worlds. Baal is in the *Challenger,* and the *Challenger* is in Baal; religion is in technology; the pagan god is in the rocket; the rocket is in the statue; the rocket on its launching pad is in the ancient idol—and our sophisticated knowledge is in our archaic fascinations. In short, the construction of a failed or successful society is in the successful or failed project of going toward the stars.

The object becomes what I call in *The Parasite* a quasi object, which traces or makes visible the relations that constitute the group through which it passes, like the token in a children's game. A quasi object that nonetheless remains a useful technical object, even a high-tech one, directed toward the physical world. It often happens that the most sophisticated tools play their main role socially but without losing their objective purpose.

BL So, we never have only one pole—that of the object or of the subject— but at least two?

MS It seems to me that this is a great, magnificent story, an epic with double access. Perhaps we no longer know how to narrate because we're unable to stitch together what happens at the rocket-launching station at Kourou and what happens, for example, at Lourdes. Plato stitched together effortlessly the story of the downfall of the shepherd Gyges with contemporary navigation and geometry. (We have Saint Bernadette in her grotto at Lourdes, and what philosopher would dare to talk about her in the way that *The Republic* describes the statue of the horse in the crevasse?) In devoting myself to the task of stitching, I dream of translating (with good reason) the immense word *phenomenology* by the expression "the apparition speaks." In this we are both in the realm of philosophy and in the grotto of miracles.

But I am not dreaming when I displace the genius of Copernican or Galilean philosophy of knowledge in the direction of Kepler. The latter describes the planets as circulating in an elliptical orbit with two centers—the sun, brilliant and fiery, and a second, dark one that is never spoken about. Indeed, knowledge has two centers; by its gigantic movement the Earth shows us the double pole. Need I keep showing this, or describing it?

I speak with great pleasure of this sewing and this overcast seam, since the last narrative I published (yes, it's a narrative) has as its theme a meditation on the bond—the bond of the *Contract*, to be exact.

BL So, this is a way of approaching your works in a constructive way, but the reader must first accept the idea that there is no modern world, that in fact there never has been . . .

MS Admittedly, our predecessors knew how to read these two elements of Ju-Piter—no doubt better than we do—but they did not know the full import of them. We know these more clearly. This modern work of analysis has been useful and incomparable.

BL Yes, but wait a minute. This modern world did not have those ingredients by itself. When I say that we have never been modern, I mean that, because of your work, we realize in retrospect that our societies have never held together thanks only to the social scientists' collective. That they have never held together thanks only to the natural scientists' objects. This is why I spoke of a parenthesis. It is not because of the Copernican revolution that we have held together, that the West has developed. The object has always been in the middle. It is not divided in two at all; it never was. This is a Copernican counterrevolution.

MS To my mind Kepler is a better model than Copernicus.

BL This enormous circulation of objects around the two centers has always constituted the collective. The modern, Copernican construction has never existed on its own.

MS It organizes a sort of lack of education. Neither sciences nor humanities—just information. Thermodynamics, materials mechanics, computer science: unknown; Baal: unknown. Thus, we learn everything about the rocket, through what the usual networks announce about it. Perhaps we could use this distancing from the sciences and tradition to define news reporting, or information in the ordinary sense.

And this information will henceforth serve as the basis for philosophical theories, won't it? Fairly recently, this was the price paid for the exclusivity of the social sciences: the substitution of information for knowledge.

BL It's mythology. It's the very beautiful expression you often use: "There is no pure myth except the idea of a science that is pure of all myth."

MS That dates from my youth, at the Ecole Normale, where it was said that the true work of philosophy consisted of purifying science of all myths. That seemed to me to define aptly a certain religion: washing the hands before entering sacred places, which were themselves perfectly pure or purified by shining waters—the separation of the sacred and the profane.

The more one tries to exclude myth, the more it returns in force, since it is founded on the operation of exclusion. And, on the other hand, how can one understand or practice any science whatsoever without using an excluded third party?

At Philosophy's Blind Spot, Everything Begins Again

BL To conclude this session I'd like to clarify things a bit more, at the risk of simplification. Correct me if I'm wrong. There is the pole of nature, that of Ju-, *as we have said, or of the* Challenger—*in other words, science and technology. And then there is the pole of* Piter *or of* Baal—*that of the collective. Here our first problem arises. These two poles were put in place in a radical way by Kant, since in the middle is the phenomenon. Now Kant places the individual* subject *at the other pole, and we contemporaries place the* collective *there. For you this doesn't make any difference?*

MS It's no narrow paradox that Descartes places the *ego* of *cogito* at the center of knowledge at the very moment when science begins—that is, at the very moment a collectivity begins to form, still nonprofessionally, organizing for demonstrations and experimentation. In other words, as soon as science begins, the subject is immediately collective. Look at the Greek schools of mathematics—they only grew in proportion to the advancement of the history of science. And, again, there's no narrow paradox in the great enterprise of founding knowledge on a transcendental subjectivity—on another cogito, that of Kant—more than a century later, at the time when science became more professional, in an immense movement of collectivization.

In science only the collective *we* can know things. The individual *I* sometimes invents, but how the community of researchers is wary of it! In the same way that the church abhors mystics. I sense that here, on the question of debate, you are often going to get the better of me.

BL The philosophy of science in this century—in the United States with Kuhn, in Germany with Habermas, in France with the sociology of science—has taken its time about replacing the knowing subject with a knowing collectivity.

MS It's too bad. We spend all our time correcting simple artifacts. But, on the other hand, what a change! The collective *we* does not function in the same way as the individual *I*—far from it. In any case they are both equally difficult to understand.

BL Let's call this position subjective/collective.

MS All right.

BL We could even remove the subject, or the collective, and replace it with structures, with epistemes, functions, language ("ça parle"), etc. None of this would change anything. In the middle is the tmesis, or the chiasm you were speaking of.

MS How could it be otherwise, my dear Socrates?

BL Now I'm trying to situate you in opposition to the tasks of critical philosophy. For this I divide Kepler's ellipse in two. Above, there is the greater and greater effort to separate myth that is pure of any science from science that is pure of any myth. And, now, what's most entertaining is to superimpose what's happening in the world on this effort of purification by the philosophers. Now, then, the quasi objects, the hybrids, the monsters, the Baal-Challengers, the Ju-Piters multiply—a first, second, third industrial revolution. Each time the quasi objects multiply and the philosophers render more and more unthinkable . . .

MS . . . what is happening before our very eyes.

BL On the one hand, you have the philosophical enterprise, on the other, the multiplication of quasi objects—the exact opposite. As a result, we can see very clearly the function of your books.

MS I had always imagined that their purpose was obviously to understand the world in which we live. I was not totally convinced of it, of course, and perhaps that is why I was not able to persuade my contemporaries. You take a weight off my mind, and I thank you for having converted me to debate.

BL It's always necessary to situate oneself, precisely, in this intermediary position.

MS This is the blind spot of all philosophy for the last three hundred years.

BL It's the juncture, but the juncture of the two extremes. Now it's here that your theory of mingling is so important, because you never imagine it as a mingling of pure forms. This was, nonetheless, Kant's very idea—to purify the two poles enough so that their reunion, the phenomenon, would be conceived as a perfectly determined mingling of the pure forms of the object and the pure forms of the subject. But you go in an entirely different direction.

MS The Natural Contract scandalizes people for the same reason. Since nature is an object, how can it be the partner in a contract?

I'm faithfully pursuing the project of mingling. Notice the title of *Les Cinq sens: philosophie des corps mêlés, vol. 1* [The Five Senses: Philosophy of Mixed Bodies, vol. 1]. You have only to add to all my other books "volume 2," "volume 3," and so on.

BL This is why the postmodernists cannot understand The Natural Contract *any more than they can understand your other books. Nature, which is now seen as something to be protected rather than dominated, has no thinkable place for them. In the modern thought going on around us there is no longer any place for an anthropogenic nature. It's an incomprehensible hybrid. And so we have to start again from scratch, at new costs.*

MS This is the source of Ju-Piter's *parabole.*

BL Indeed, it is a very enlightening parable/parabola.

MS I have never ceased to inhabit it.

BL But, for you, at the center there are some interesting things.

MS Everything that is interesting.

BL And this profoundly changes our conception of history, because you reutilize the past differently. The past no longer has the outdated character that the succession of radical revolutions gave to it. You place yourself in the midst of it all. There is a history of things. So, things are not aligned on the side of a pole of Nature—this is the most amazing aspect of your research. When you criticize a-cosmicism, you don't come back to the object. For you the object is active, socialized, something to which a lot of bizarre things happen. On the other hand, for you society does not have the characteristics attributed to it by the social sciences. It is once again filled with things.

MS Humanity begins with things; animals don't have things.

BL The misunderstanding is complete.

MS But, if there is a source of renewal, it must be there.

BL It is there.

MS So, who hid this treasure?

Wisdom

Bruno Latour: In our preceding conversations we addressed certain difficulties in reading your work, and I allowed myself to "put you through the ordeal," as you said, of asking you to situate yourself in relation to currents of philosophical thought and in relation to your contemporaries. You reproached me for interrogating you too much on your earliest books, and on professional relations, and not enough on your recent books and on what interests you today, which you call your morality.

Michel Serres: Indeed, questions of analysis and method interest me less today than in the past. What philosophy seeks, perhaps most of all, is wisdom. Science and reason are part of this but not all of it—far from it.

The word *sapiens,* which the Romans used to translate the Greek *sage,* and which anthropology took in order to define man, derives from a verb that means having taste, subtly sensing flavors and aromas.

Wisdom and Philosophy

BL I was always taught to distinguish philosophy—which argues, studies, and doubts—from wisdom, which is too moralizing, too aesthetic, and also too self-satisfied. I thought that philosophy sought or loved wisdom without ever possessing it.

MS Who's talking about definitive possession? We should beware of distinctions that don't give us the choice, without even hiding the fact that they separate good from bad—in this case research and doubt from self-satisfaction.

BL Perhaps my problem is that you have not yet given us your definition of philosophy.

MS Philosophy composes a world, *in its totality, or in general, and in its most minute detail.* It seeks and gives answers not only to problems that are "expert" (and often narrowly professional) about art or science—space, time, history and knowledge, methods and demonstrations—but also, and perhaps especially, it gives answers to simple and inevitable, vital questions that we all ask, starting in childhood, and that never have been answered except through philosophy. Questions like what is the truth about individual and collective death, about violence (addressed in "Thanatocracy"); about the body, skin, the senses, life at home and on the road *(Les Cinq sens);* about the sea, the sky, trees, poverty *(Detachment);* about gardens, volcanoes, rocks, milestones, clothing *(Statues);* about animals, our relations to our closest neighbors, to work, meals, sickness *(The Parasite);* about the land, cities, the law, justice, the planet Earth *(The Natural Contract);* about rivers, mountains, love, youth, education *(Le Tiers-Instruit);* about others, exile, old age, friendship—about virtue, yes, and about goodness too, but also about evil, especially about evil, which never ceases.

May these questions never cease and, like the pieces of a mosaic, may they fill all of existence and all that can be thought about, from a blade of grass to the fate of the gods, but, especially, may the answers come less from books that are read and recited or from a packet of index cards than from direct and often painful experience of the state of things. Whoever does not construct a world—place by place, object by object, faithfully, with his hands, with his own flesh, creating a totality—is devoting himself not so much to philosophy as to criticism, logic, history, etc.

BL But this work, which I can understand, does not necessarily lead to wisdom.

MS Before you can invent a wisdom you must first construct this total world, immersed in the problem of evil. Or, even more difficult, wouldn't it be better to create a kind of wise man, a sage, alive and concretely capable of being educated? No doubt each generation would revise his image, intentionally or not.

We are familiar with the image of the sage that preceded us; the one who follows him bears no resemblance to him. For today we are living through a very curious and important inversion of the sage's image.

BL I don't understand what transformation you are speaking of. Perhaps I lived through it without realizing it, and this is why for me "the sage" does not seem current.

MS Since you ask, here is what preceded our current day. Submitting to irremediable laws, we have always lived in an unforgiving world. Wisdom—whether age-old, classical, Christian, secular, or even recent—helped us to bear our inevitable pains, which were produced by a necessity *independent of us.*

From our beginnings we had regulated our actions on this distinction between *things that depended on us and those that in no way depended on us.*

The local—the near, the neighboring, the adjoining, the next-door—sometimes depended on us, but the spatially distant, the distant future, the Earth, the universe, humanity, matter, life, all the global categories that philosophers theorize about, always eluded our influence.

BL But we still inhabit this same world of necessity. *How can we escape from it?*

MS Does your sweet youth prevent you from seeing the recent change?

Suddenly, toward the middle of the century, at the end of World War II, we have the rise in power of all the mixed scientific disciplines—physics, biology, medicine, pharmacology—plus the whole set of technologies brought about by them. We are finally truly effective in the organization of work, in providing food, in matters of sexuality, of illness, in the hope of prolonging life—in short, in everyday life, intimate and collective. Further, we are finally the masters of space, of matter, and of life. All of this has pushed back the limits and almost eliminated what *does not depend on us.* We have found ways to lessen fatigue, to practically abolish need and pain, to avoid inevitable distress. So, what remains irremediable?

Preserved, appeased, practically anesthetized, two or three generations of the West (no doubt for the first time in history) have just lived like gods, in the happy and safe certitude that, henceforth, everything *depended*—if not immediately, at least in the short term—on their knowledge or their technical achievements.

While the old global necessity was collapsing, they devoted themselves, in security, to the intoxication of a growing consumerism that reached new heights of consumption, and they experienced the ensuing crisis in everyday morality, which had obviously become useless and incomprehensible.

With rockets, satellites, television, and fax machines, we dominate gravity and space. Tomorrow we will be able to choose the sex of our children (which we will no longer bear unless we are assured of their normality) ... whereas the force of gravity, distance, our planet's place in the solar system, hereditary diseases, and procreation have always been considered as natural things, independent of us.

So, here we are, masters even of things that used to hold us in subjection. Death itself is pushed back, and old age is rejuvenated. Life's briefness, wept over or sung by the ancient sages, has been succeeded by calculations of its expectancy, which, for wealthy women in wealthy countries, exceeds seventy years. Our wisdom is shaken by the tearing down of those objective dependencies that were formerly irremediable and unforgiving.

BL Do you mean that, since wisdom is a technique of survival, the fact that the frontiers of necessity have been pushed back makes it superficial, almost old-fashioned?

MS Exactly. Individuals and groups of people crushed by irremediable pains live in my childhood memories and in the memory (now nearly illegible) of the humanities. At that time moral virtues formed a system of practical recipes (more or less effective) for resisting the bondage dealt us by the world and our debility. We no longer need such crutches.

This is really the end of a history, at least for the richest inhabitants of well-off nations. But the third and fourth worlds remain immersed in the era of my childhood and of the humanities.

BL So, then, science and technology remove the distinction upon which morals are based?

MS Their recent achievements, at any rate. The old adage changes and becomes: "Everything depends or will depend on us, someday." Better yet: "Everything itself will depend on us; not just all things, but systems as such, and totalities." So, what can we do? The answer: given enough time, anything, or almost, globally speaking, since our science and technology have discovered *(and this is what's totally new)* some of the paths that go from what's next door, or neighboring, toward totality, from the local to the global. Certainly.

But even this is disturbing and suddenly turns back upon itself. So, again, what can we do? Answer: given enough time, anything, and in quantity, indeed, twice as much, but what about quality? We are capable of all the good in the world, certainly: feeding, caring, healing. But, diametrically, we are capable of blowing up the planet, disturbing its climate, choosing to give birth only to baby boys or only to baby girls, of creating in our laboratories deadly viruses that are transmissible at the will of the winds. We have become the tragic deciders of life or death, masters of the greatest aspects of our former dependence: Earth, life and matter, time and history, good and evil. We have encroached upon the theories of metaphysics.

This new mastery has made old necessity change camps. Whereas it formerly inhabited nature, either inert or living, and slept, hidden, in the laws of the world, now, in the last fifty years, it has decamped surreptitiously, to take its place right inside our mastery. It now inhabits our freedom.

We are now, admittedly, the masters of the Earth and of the world, but our very mastery seems to escape our mastery. We have all things in hand, but we do not control our actions. Everything happens as though our powers escaped our powers—whose partial projects, sometimes good and often intentional, can backfire or unwittingly cause evil. As far as I know, we do not yet control the unexpected road that leads from the local pavement, from good intentions, toward a possible global hell.

Our conquests outstrip our deliberate intentions. Observe, in fact, the acceleration in the trajectories of our technological advances. No sooner is it announced that something is *possible* than it is in part *achieved,* propelled down the slope of competition, imitation, or interest. It is almost as quickly considered *desirable,* and by the next day it is *necessary:* people will go to court if they are deprived of it. The fabric of our history is woven today of these immediate passages from possibility to reality, from contingency to necessity.

BL But this is the classical theme of the sorcerer's apprentice or the even more classical one of the spiritual emptiness that accompanies materialism. "Our technology outstrips us." What is there in this that is new for philosophy's contemplation?

MS Let's not be sidetracked by old images. The newness comes from these successful passages from the local to the global.

Let's summarize this segment of our contemporary odyssey. After the sciences of quantity came those of quality, as we said, and then those of relations, which I described earlier. Now we are attaining the sciences of modalities, which are the *possible,* the *actual,* the *contingent,* the *necessary.* Thus, we no longer live in the world's necessity but in the modalities of a knowledge that, further, bears the only future project of our societies. We are following the blind fate of sciences whose technology invents possibilities that immediately become necessities.

So, it no longer depends on us that everything depends on us. This is the new principle or foundation of the new wisdom.

BL Necessity returns, but in the form of the impossibility of our not deciding everything. *Are we forced into total mastery?*

MS Yes, *we will be able* to choose the sex of our children; genetics, biochemistry, physics, and their related technologies give us the necessary power, but *we will be obliged* to administer this power, which for the moment seems to elude us, because it goes faster and farther than we are able to foresee or control, beyond our desires to redirect it, our will to decide about it, our freedom to manage it. We have resolved the Cartesian question: "How can we dominate the world?" Will we know how to resolve the next one: "How can we dominate our domination; how can we master our own mastery?"

BL So, it's an infinite freedom, like Sartre's, but which, unlike his, inevitably extends to the details of every science and technology?

MS Let's not get sidetracked by quotations. All of this means that we *must* choose the sex of our children, that we *must* verify their normality before they are born, that we must maintain the balance of the world, that we must organize or protect all forms of life ... without realizing it, we pass from the verb *can* to the verb *must*, with regard to the same actions. What an unexpected return of morality!

The generations before us rejoiced, briefly, in declining the verb *can;* our generation finds itself forced to conjugate the verb *must.* Thus, we find ourself suddenly under a new yoke.

BL But this argument still doesn't resolve the split between philosophy and wisdom.

MS As a result, this split certainly exists, but at the same time it disappears: wisdom and philosophy come together on either side of these two or three exceptional, godlike generations in Western history. Necessity admittedly has lost the battle; we have triumphed over it, objectively—but the same war continues against necessity. Only its front has changed. What a strange new development: necessity inhabits the same camp as our freedom!

Necessity abandons nature and joins society. It has left *things* and reconquered mankind's home. Being masters imposes crushing responsibilities, suddenly driving us far from the independence we so recently believed would henceforth be the bed of roses of our new powers.

From now on we are steering things that, in the past, we didn't steer. In dominating the planet, we become accountable for it. In manipulating death, life, reproduction, the normal and the pathological, we become responsible for them. *We are going to have to decide about every thing, and even about Everything*—about the physical and thermodynamic future, about Darwinian evolution, about life, about the Earth and about time, about filtering *possibilities*—candidates to be evaluated for becoming *realities*—a process Leibniz described as characterizing the work of God the creator, in the secret of his infinite understanding.

Thus, we are going to need a prodigious knowledge, sharpened in every detail, harmonious in its broad workings, and a sovereign wisdom—clear-sighted regarding the present and prudent regarding the future. Is this divinity?

For the world suddenly seems to place itself under the workings or the competence of our collective laws. We used to have a hard time conceiving of the existence of objective laws, independent of our human and political laws. Today these objective laws return and are part of the rules of the city. Will the Earth depend upon the city?—will the physical world depend upon the political world?

The lives and actions of our children soon will be conditioned, in fact, by an Earth that we will have programmed, decided upon, produced, and modeled. Thus, we find the consequences of our conquests weighing on our shoulders, as conditions of our future decisions. A new kind of feedback—no doubt the result of our global powers—turns practical action inside-out, like the finger of a glove. In the future, we will live only under the conditions that we will have produced in this era.

An Objective Morality

BL So, if I understand rightly, we must no longer separate morality from philosophy, as before, because morality is passing from the individual and the subject—from what he can control—to the object, which he is obliged to control?

MS Yes. So, the first foundation or the first condition of wisdom resides in the ensemble of objective facts produced by knowledge. The technology of reality makes the consequences of our acts into the conditions of our survival. We construct the givens.

BL So, we believe ourselves to be freer than the ancients, but we are actually less so?

MS This is the reason for the melancholy songs whose *continuo* of nostalgia we hear so often today. Essentially, our predecessors must have lived fairly tranquilly in the era of the old natural necessity, in spite of its exorbitant price in pain, famine, death from disease, and short life. One had only to direct oneself or, according to one's role, to direct a few people, sometimes far away but more often close. Even Emperor Marcus Aurelius of Rome, ancient master of a fragmented world, did not carry the burdens of the entire Earth on his shoulders—although he claimed to—nor the burden of Life itself. Now we find his moral obligations light. Ours weigh megatons.

He was not even accountable for his body. Once I know (via scientific probability) the consequences of a certain kind of work or a certain food or some prescribed exercise, I become largely responsible for my illnesses and even for my death. As a product of objective knowledge, morality dislodges my very cultural background; I have to substitute for my usual ways, for my deliciously blind regional habit of enjoying local dishes dripping with alcohol, fats, and sugar, a certain dietetic and austere obligation—in fact, the microscopic, temperate virtue of limiting myself to a salad! And I must run quickly from there to the gym. Illness and death are now my responsibility.

Gluttony, laziness, lust, and anger pass from the confessional to the laboratory, from spiritual and subjective intention to rational evidence and obligation, both final and causal. By creating a communal pool of pathogens, individual sexual freedom has turned into collective viral necessity. This or that local act sets off a global condition of survival.

BL So, I was wrong in thinking that morality would bring us back to the self-centeredness of the individual subject?

MS Evaluate the outline and general scope, the *obviously objective aspect* of wisdom springing from the era when necessity co-habits with freedom, instead of opposing it. Wisdom abandons the individual body, leaving a few derisory but noteworthy examples, and invades the collective and the world, even historical time, because science and technology make us responsible for the generations to come, for their numbers and their health as well as the real conditions that we will leave them—this or that kind of a world, depending on our decisions and our acts. Successful scientific practice *objectifies* wisdom.

Let me stress: *When necessity decamps from the objective world and moves toward people, morality, in turn, moves from individual people toward the objective world.*

For what reasons must I behave in one way and not in another? So that the Earth can continue, so that the air remains breathable, so that the sea remains the sea. What are the reasons for some other necessity? So that time continues to flow, so that life continues to propagate itself, with comparable chances of multiplicity. Quite simply and objectively.

BL So, duty is no longer a categorical imperative of practical reason, as Kant said? It can also be deduced from pure reason? Cause and law, which have been so rigorously distinguished from each other, are no longer distinct?

MS In general, why *must* I do something? So that the cause remains and can give rise to the cause. Be-cause.

Why is there duty? Because we are becoming the guardians, the conservators, the promoters of *cause*'s entire existence, local and global. Physically, objectively. Why this or that obligation? So that life survives. Biologically at least, if nothing more.

Must equals cause. Duty is the same as cause, since the consequences of our actions rejoin their conditions. *Because the causes or the objects that we produce give birth to us too, in a network of causes.* Because, spawned by us, our actions become our mothers. We are our own ancestors, Adam and Eve, through the intermediary of the Earth and of life, which we mold almost at our leisure.

Must equals cause, because we have become the authors of ongoing creation. Because necessity has reached our dwelling place. Because there it has married our freedom. Because in universal history we are the first offspring of this marriage.

Because our scientific and technological powers make our transcendence flow continually toward and in and for immanence. Here is the name of our new ethos: *Natura sive homines*—Nature, meaning human culture; human morality, meaning the objective laws of Nature.

So, morality is coherent with the philosophy of law expressed in *The Natural Contract.*

BL *But this impression of mastery that makes morality objective is paradoxical. Necessity has never seemed so rigorous. Are the armor-plated laws of development any more flexible, for most people, than ancient fate?*

MS Like the tail of a comet, throwbacks or continuations of ancient objective necessity still linger—misery, hunger, and diseases, both new and residual, ravaging the third and fourth worlds, growing exponentially. And those who should be held accountable—those living in the brilliant head of the comet, leaving this abject misery in their wake and multiplying it—are the very ones (and I am one of them) who seek this wisdom. This is a second responsibility, a new obligation, more conditions issuing from the results of our actions—the latest blow to the collective narcissism of the wealthy nations.

BL The second foundation or the second condition of wisdom resides in the whole set of human causes produced by our powers—financial, political, strategic, juridical, administrative, geomediative, and, in the last analysis, overall, essentially scientific.

MS The technology of humanity turns these social products of our acts into conditions of survival, thus putting us under obligation. We are the masters of the Earth, and we are constructing a world that is almost universally miserable and that is becoming the objective, founding *given* of our future.

BL Two or three generations, mine perhaps more than yours, have profited to the hilt from this waning of necessity, but, if I understand rightly, the party is over?

MS The party celebrating the end of the old necessity—a party that was admittedly legitimate, but often repugnant, with an orgy of riches, intoxication with diverse drugs, with ongoing, trumped-up spectacles—is now followed by the dawn of a new settling of accounts, in which necessity returns, through a private entrance, behind us, inside the concept of "us."

Measure the road we have traveled since epistemology, which only wanted to debate about methods and demonstrations. Would you call self-centered, for example, this obligation—this ensemble of bonds, of *liens* (in the etymological sense)—that tie us to the third world? Have you noticed that we've never pronounced the pronoun *I*—that we only speak of *us?*

The Humanities Forgotten

BL I still don't see how you are going to found your morality. It seems like placing all our hopes in the social sciences, but you don't believe in them, and you must admit that you usually say bad things about them.

MS In those truly revolutionary times (I'm referring to the rapid transformation of the outcomes of our actions into conditions for our next actions, and the transformation of *can* into *must*), our reliance and my hopes were on the social sciences. I say this because the greatest blind spot came from this *us*—so efficient and sovereign, launched like a great ship, swift, powerful, and heavy, into the heaving sea, and which the duty officer could only vaguely steer, since he could not know the array of constraints weighing on his decisions nor integrate them fast enough.

Still, this old cybernetic metaphor for politics is becoming so weak as to almost fade away, since in the current reality the successive directions of the *gouvernail,* or rudder, change the state of the sea itself, and the volume of the vessel. Nonetheless, I retain this metaphor, since the sailors of yesteryear are the only ones who remember that you can't reach your destination with just one sea-mark; you need at least two—it's an error to take only one alignment reading, in a single direction.

For example, question the claims of biomedical ethics when they say they seek the patient's "enlightened consent." What "enlightenment" do they advise? At least two sources of light are necessary; if not, what's presented is simply a position, which rapidly becomes a directive that is imperialistic, necessary, obligatory. In this case the enlightenment comes only from the doctor, from the expert, the researcher, the biologist—in short, always and only from science. And the patient who must decide, in haste and in the midst of a situation that is often distressing, knows only the fate of the new necessity (as blind as the preceding one), that of technological or rational egoism.

The light that depends on us mingles intimately with what does not depend on us—the shadow that I spoke of earlier. Interestingly, the maximum amount of light can result in the maximum amount of shadow. We need another beacon. Which explains the recourse, first, to the social sciences, whose efforts explore precisely this *us* which, paradoxically, no longer depends on us.

BL So, the social sciences are necessary in order to make other compass readings, in order to triangulate, to reach our destination?

MS These new sciences (which were enjoying their own party) taught us a thousand things and even a new way of thinking. From linguistics to the history of religion, from anthropology to geography, we are indebted to them for important information, without which we would remain in the dark about a plurality of worlds. They have drawn us into a general, even universal, tolerance, into an almost ethereal pliability that makes us astonished at the opinionated dogmas that our fathers found rigorous. Our philosophy of the hard sciences itself could no longer exist without the social sciences.

This being said, each light carries its related shadow. Just as illuminations from the hard sciences finally fall into the blindness of this effective *us* whose inertia grows with its mass and acceleration—that is, into the need for the social sciences—so the latter teach us nothing when they remain estranged from each and every object, if they only explore the relations between men and ignore the things of the world.

The best light is obtained in the mingled region of interferences between the two sources, and this region vanishes if the two flows have no common intersection. If each center claims to be the sole source of light, outside of which there is nothing but obscurantism, then the only compass readings or pathways obtained are those of obedience.

BL So, morality would be obtained from a mingling, a marriage, a complement between the hard sciences, which would have to be pushed toward society, and the social sciences, which would have to be pushed toward the world of objects?

MS Certainly. This being said, the game, then, was not one for two players, but for three. And recently the main struggle was not between the hard sciences and the social sciences, since both were sciences (real or self-designated) and ignored each other superbly (the one, a world without people; the other, people without a world). War supposes some relations. No, the main struggle was between these two and what they claimed to replace—the humanities. This seemingly secondary but nonetheless crucial game was taken up again in the preceding decades by the forgetting of necessity.

We need to understand how the godlike generations of happy consumption lost sight of the old problem of evil. Once they were seated at the feast of immortality, drunk with ambrosia, tasting the mastery of earthly woes in the new Garden of Earthly Delights, how could they still tarry over the memory of misfortune, over the message of the Pyramids, with their terrifying provisions for the journey into the desertlike space of death? How could they dwell on the lamentations of the prophet Jeremiah on the ruins of the city or on the account of Job, howling from his dung heap, shard in hand and scratching his boils? No more could they linger over the monotone terrors of the Trojan War, over the wanderings of Ulysses, buffeted by the winds, over the tragic Greeks and the punishment of Prometheus, god of primitive apprenticeship, over the passion of Jesus Christ, crucified on the Cross, over the martyrs and sacrifices related in the golden legends of the Christian saints. They could not abide the accounts and scenes, sung or painted, of the great human passions and sufferings—that immense, continuing clamor, moaning, and lamentation, the psalm of mankind, weeping over the absurd, vain and uselessly mortal drama of its own ineradicable violence—a low and timid lamentation, continuous, barely audible, absolutely beautiful, and the source of all beauty, unable to make itself heard because the furor of violence, the noise of vengeance—absolutely ugly and the source of all mediocrity—always drowns it out. How could they still tarry over this music, this voice, this moaning preserved by the cultures of woe from which we sprang—trans-historic background noise that cannot be attributed to anyone, but springs from the sum of humanity, from the exasperatingly tight cords of history, or from the unity of God? Those at the feast said to themselves, "What's the point of preserving what from now on is useless?"

Just as the hard sciences go their way without man, thereby risking becoming inhumane, just as the social sciences go theirs with neither world nor object, thereby exposing themselves to irresponsibility, likewise, in aggregate and in parallel, in the name of a science that is finally efficient and lucid, the two disciplines together impose the forgetting of the humanities—that continuous cry of suffering, that multiple and universal expression, in every language, of human misfortune. Our short-term powers scorn our long-term frailties.

It's said that the ancient gods laughed during the feast of the immortals, replete with narcotics, deaf to the lamentations of mortals. Are we about to leave Olympus now, when it was only our parents who reached it? Worn out with dreary overeating, we entertain ourselves in the evening, on the screens of televisions spread over our mountain of abundance and money, by watching millions of skeletal people die. More than our brothers, are they our children, or, rather, our products? Even more, are they the necessary conditions of our future life? And thus our parents?

Here, again, the wide and deep schism will give way to a suture, for in order to understand the new, new world (the one in which necessity rejoins freedom), the light emanating from those ancient texts becomes crucial, because of the long experience they reveal with the aforementioned necessity. A single source of light is not enough—neither that of the hard sciences nor the exclusive light of the social sciences, since they both claim to be scientific.

BL This brings us again to the movement we talked about in our last conversation. The humanities bear within them the question of the hyphen. It's no longer a matter of opposing the physical sciences to the social sciences but of adding to them that which joins them—the Gordian knot, which should never again be cut.

MS Could ideology, whose demise is much talked of, perhaps be defined simply as a philosophy that takes its values and foundations exclusively from the information provided by the so-called social sciences, or one that, inversely, takes them exclusively from the so-called hard sciences, as though using only one source of light? Reciprocally, can any thought conditioned by only one of these sources be considered as ideological? What ideology are we bowing down before when we give the experts the "enlightened consent" they demand?

In sum, the objective causes produced by the hard sciences establish a first wisdom, which must be founded anew on human events, which are also produced by us, are also conditions of our acts.

But this only makes one foundation—that of the sciences in general. Now, two foundations are as necessary as are two sources of light.

Like *can* and *must, knowledge* and *misfortune* cannot be separated; each is as objective and no doubt universal as the other. By only knowing or living one of them, we are unaware of what we think, what we do, and what we are.

If we could speak every language and decipher every code, if we were informed by absolute knowledge, we would know nothing without at most, the experience of—or, at least, hearkening to— this suffering that is without remission and without end and whose oceanic clamor produces the background noise from which all our knowledge and the conditions of our practical activities spring.

This is the origin of knowledge and our expertise. No, we did not set out long ago to understand things and act upon their future because we felt and observed through the five senses, the way philosophy once amused itself by saying we did, or for other reasons just as cold. No—we did it because we suffered from our misery or our crimes, and because we were moved by the intuition of our untimely death. Knowledge is based on this mourning.

Our capacities come from our weaknesses, and our effectiveness from our fragilities. Our science has no other foundation than this permanent collapse, this lack, this endless slippage into an abyss of pain.

The problem of evil underlies the power we derive from our various means of addressing it. This is why it always reappears, a not-unexpected sire, in our exercise of this power. Spawned by it, science begins with it, rests on it, partly resolves and partly rediscovers it, is engaged with it in these myriad loops of solutions and ensuing conversations that today constitute the greatest part of our history, the struggle behind the anxieties that follow our triumphs, and the victories that succeed our anguish. Nothing is more important than remembering this genesis, which is forgotten by philosophy itself.

The last people who still keep vigil over what are rightly called the humanities are the guardians of human pain, transported from age to age by the geniuslike voice of the wisest ancestors of our scientists. Don't exclude this ancestral rumor from decisions or from apprenticeship; from this the "expert" logos was slowly formed, and at the first sign of trouble it is to this that you will run to seek vital advice, as you would to an experienced ancestor.

If you drive away tragedy, it will come back tomorrow, of your own creation, since your expertise is born of it. And if you have forgotten or wiped out this deposit, you will no longer know how to domesticate the tragedies of the day, unchanging since the world was born, nor how to live again on an Earth and in a history from which misfortune has not disappeared.

Deprived of the terrible lessons emanating from this source, the sciences would train our eminent experts to become brutes and savages, infinitely more dangerous (as our century has abundantly shown) than during the days when necessity dominated our paltry and ineffectual technologies. The future will force experts to come quickly to the humanities and to humanity, there to seek a science that is *humane*—since in our language the word signifying our genus also signifies compassion.

As a result, what is philosophy? The irrepressible witness of universal misfortune before an absolute knowledge that, without this *instruction* (in the multiple senses of origin, pedagogy, and law), would be the equivalent of irresponsible ignorance, whose naïveté would reconstruct a new world without forgiveness.

No Morality without Pedagogy

BL It's true that the human sciences are tragically separate from the hard sciences and, as a result, remain estranged from our times.

MS You deplore it, as I do, and you are devoted, more than I, to constructing new relations between the two. The old morality of "commitment" was a paradoxical example of estrangement from its world; it supposed the question to be resolved, without giving itself the means to resolve it. In fact, anyone who was not involved in hard science was not committed at all, even if he joined a political party, since the latter mainly repeated outdated dogmas and behaviors, whereas scientific and technological transformations were producing the contemporary era.

Our predecessors were divided with an ax blow into two parties: scientists, and denigrators of the Western reason that gave rise to science. At the interface of the ax blow, I call my hero "le Tiers-Instruit"—"the Instructed Third," or "the Troubadour of Knowledge." This gives first of all a time frame to this hybrid, or mestizo offspring of the two cultures, for, if the scientist is still young (science's knowledge is rarely more than ten years old) and the humanist is several thousand years old (receiving and transmitting ancient traditions), then the troubadour of knowledge, who is of both science and letters, has some chance of instituting the age of adulthood for which we hope.

He is admittedly a rationalist, but he does not believe that all the requirements of reason are met by science. He tempers one with the other. Likewise, he never sees the social sciences as exhausting the content transmitted by the humanities—far from it. So, for him there is as much rigor in a myth or a work of literature as in a theorem or an experiment and, inversely, as much myth in these as in literature.

BL So, to found a morality we must return to the humanities?

MS I prefer *renaissance,* rather than *return,* which always has a caricatural aspect I dislike. So, this troubadour of knowledge will become instructed in political philosophy from Shakespeare and Bodin, in sociology (why not?) from Balzac or Zola, and in linguistics by practicing style. But most of all he will learn about misfortune, in all areas. Wisdom requires us to invent a third curriculum, which will weave the warp of the rediscovered humanities to the woof of expert exactitude.

BL You still haven't really answered my question about wisdom. You've moved on to pedagogy.

MS One can never invent an abstract wisdom without first seeking to train a real and living wise man, a sage. What difference does it make if I am one, if my successors do not become wise men? The real difference between men and God, if He exists, must be that He created the world of things and the diversity of humankind by omnipotence and omniscience, whereas we, for the moment, create children whose bodies and spirits are unpredictable, in an unpredictable world. All we have is education to make us adaptably prepared for the future. When you don't have foresight—that is, providence—there remains forethought; when you don't have science there remains wisdom.

But, obliged as we are to produce more and more of the future, and to continually have it crop up again as conditions, our era is disastrously lacking in a program of instruction and education. And no one has ever been able to elaborate such a program without first sketching the profile of the person to be educated.

So, here is his body, for which he is responsible, by diet and exercise. And here is his hybrid "third culture," illuminated from two sources. Beauty is located at the intersection of these clarities. Beauty *saves* as much as science does; it is as objective as science. I don't know which life is a greater failure, the one lacking beauty or the one lacking science. Have you noticed the instructive parallel between ugliness and sterility? Even fecundity or the art of invention cannot do without beauty.

This is why *Le Tiers-Instruit* describes a Keplerian revolution with, precisely, a double source: there is the sun of knowledge, and, at a measurable distance, there is a second center—at least as active, though less dazzling. We would be wrong in believing the circular gnoseology, centered uniquely around the source of light, as suggested by the word *research (recherche),* whose root designates a circle—or even, as suggested by the word *encyclopedia,* more learned and more transparent. No, there is in the universe a second center, at a distance from the sun. In fact, wisdom functions elliptically, as Kepler said long ago of the planetary system.

The "third curriculum" will follow Kepler's new law by measuring the constant distance between these two centers, by estimating what is owed to the one, first of all, and to the other and will seek the reasons behind this distance, will evaluate the productivity of the other sun and even its fecundity—and not simply as a matter of control or regulatory attraction but by asking what the one would lose without the other.

Weakness as a Prime Mover in History

BL I was right in being skeptical. Your portrait of a wise man leads to complete isolation, to narcissism, to the Ivory Tower. When a person speaks of morality, he is always led to concentrate on himself, which doesn't lead to very much.

MS I like your impatience, which is as lively as youth. My old age simply requests a little patience. I first had to describe the body and its powers (the five senses, if you will), then the culture (the third curriculum) of the generation growing up today, which, I believe, is inverting those of the preceding generation. Now, you are right, culture and the body are immersed in a group that in turn conditions them—this is what we're getting at. Not only does each generation define itself and choose its model, but, above all, it knows how to elect its "Other" or "Others."

BL You need to tell us who these "Others" are.

MS Perhaps no other period in history has seen so many losers and so few winners as our own. And time, because it advances through the acceleration of its exacerbated competitions and mimeticism (in science and elsewhere), produces and multiplies exponentially the great crowd of losers—of which everyone risks becoming a member, overnight—and shrinks the more and more rarefied and exclusive club (I almost said "pantheon") of winners.

What nation today, including our own, does not risk slipping into the third world? And what individual lives in the security of never falling, overnight, into the fourth world?

The small number produces the large one, which in turn conditions it. The same schema as before repeats itself. We produce the global human condition, for which we are then directly responsible. It could be said that the subject is lost in this circular objectivity, in which fortune produces misery and knowledge produces ignorance, which it nonetheless combats.

BL You are unconsciously coming back to war, which was where we started, or to the debate on debate, which we never left.

MS We cannot leave the question of evil. So, our elective Other is the loser, the weak, the frail and defenseless, the poor, the starving, the indigent without resources, those in misery with no shelter. They are now so numerous on the face of the Earth that henceforth they will give, objectively, numerically, statistically, even ontologically, the best definition of humanity—indeed, of man—reputedly so difficult to define in abstract and speculative philosophy and yet so easy to discover around oneself.

BL I no longer understand your definition of man. At the beginning of this session you were talking about Homo sapiens—*in fact, about the wise man.*

MS And what if wisdom and weakness go together? The child, the old person, the adolescent, the traveler, the migrant, the dying, the poor and the miserable, the starving, those crazed with pain, those condemned to an early death—*ecce homo,* "behold the man." There are several million of such on the planet today, according to our calculations.

And who is not weak? Power is only the boasting and lies of those who pour money into self-promotion. The winner—the powerful one, proclaimed by an assiduously circulated public morality—this victor, rare as he is, seems to our wisdom fairly bestial when he bares his teeth. In all the animal kingdom what animal is more dangerous to his fellow creatures and the Earth than the arrogant adult human male who has succeeded (as the saying goes) in competitive life? This terrifying beast can sometimes be seen passing by, briefcase in hand, in airports.

Who is the elective, essential Other? The weak. In what group does the wise man immerse himself and live? Among the weak. Henceforth you will see the sage live and think like another defenseless person, among the miserable, among those in distress throughout the entire planet.

I have wandered, have voyaged like Ulysses, who called himself No-Man and who, accordingly, became just that. I would like to say without boasting that I have known and loved Koreans, Japanese, Chinese, and Nepalis in their homelands; I have loved North, Central, and East Africans from knowing them in their own settings. I have lived for long periods in the Americas—from the hard snowdrifts of Quebec to the tropical forests of Brazil. I have been to the islands of the South Pacific, have sailed the Red Sea, and have sojourned in Singapore. I have worked in the fields like a peasant, on construction sites as a laborer; I have worked in the marketplace, even running a cash register. I'm a so-called intellectual, having gotten through the university, though fairly badly. I've rubbed elbows with ambassadors and nuns, millionaires and many indigents, geniuses (both false and authentic) and legions of imbeciles, strong men and deformed ones, drunks and obscure heroes, many humble folk and some leaders, either of countries or of other more or less important things. I have known manual laborers and smooth talkers, mystics and miscreants, the respectable and the disreputable. In short, I have insisted on passing through all latitudes and conditions, all longitudes and fortunes, from shantytowns to palaces, through all countries and occupations, all regions and neighborhoods, all languages and climates, and as authentically as I did through the diverse countries of the scientific encyclopedia—that is, by working and not as a tourist. I was even among the South American Indians, whose misery is so terrifying that one must have a heart of steel to undertake to "study" them—that is, to take something more from them, rather than immediately giving them food and drink, blankets and medicines. No, no, I have never seen nor believed what is said in books and discourses bristling with radical human differences. No—man is admittedly so diverse that you would think you were reading the entire classification of all living things, with all its branches and species, in humankind alone. But man is always and everywhere the same: wounded, full of pain, timid, fairly good overall if one looks deep enough, often pathetic—lying, mean, vicious, cruel, through weakness or lack—arrogant and dominating through error, boastful, obedient, and—if no one crushes him too much—courageous and strong, stupid and brave. On the whole he is unhappy, and, generally, statistically, globally, essentially, ontologically, objectively *pitiful.*

Finally, immersed in the midst of his fellow creatures, this wise man whose education we have described—this sage who knows but is capable of pity—does not belong solely to our time (an era in which the winners, as producers of reality and of men, henceforth are playing a game of whoever wins loses), but belongs essentially to human time and history, since weakness creates time.

BL Carried away by your criticism of dialectics, are you going to make weakness the prime mover of history?

MS As you see, I'm not afraid of generalizing. Again, courage! Yes, all human evolution passes by way of this weakness, which makes time and history—even Darwin's time, which seems to many to be the time of the victors, giving them the quasi-natural right to trample the vanquished, mute through errors. We advance through problems and not through victories, through failures and rectifications rather than by surpassing.

BL You are forgetting the great empires!

MS Not at all! The greatest powers in history only extended their empires by expelling their undesirables—their convicts, those condemned to death, prostitutes, heretics, all of the socially handicapped. Science, which will soon be the greatest empire, the most stable one in history, progresses especially, as we know, through those who are excluded from it and by the victims of its institutions. And what if Greece died from the ideology of the Olympic Games, or Rome from its growth, and what if someday we die from our competition for money and from our nuclear omnipotence? Here we have the return of the equation of *can* and *must.*

BL Are you saying that since the defeat of the ideologies and intellectual movements that claimed to defend the oppressed, we must find other ways to protect them?

MS Yes and no. Truly yes, and equally no, if it means putting ourselves in the position of protector—in other words, in the dominant position. Admittedly, henceforth the questions that are not only the most urgent but also the most philosophically essential are the following: What language do the most miserable people speak? How are the weakest to save themselves from certain death? How are the third and fourth worlds going to survive, both of which are expanding vertically and soon will make up almost the totality of the world? How can we understand the fragility of men and things—meaning the Earth and global humanity? How can we then understand the relations between knowledge and technical efficiency, power and our weaknesses? Do you see the same objective morality returning, from the other side of the universe, with a second foundation?

When I speak of the weakest I'm also talking about intellectual weakness. In the era of triumphant science, of sovereign technology, of truths communicated through global media, how can education be so degraded, how can culture collapse, how can ignorance and the number of illiterates grow so rampantly? Isn't it paradoxical that communication, through space, misses the connection because of time?

Thus, the problem of evil returns, writ large.

Objective Evil

BL By reopening the problem of evil, you want to rehabilitate one of the great philosophical or theological problems, which criticism thought it was rid of—transmitted by the humanities but believed a dead issue by the hard sciences and the social sciences?

MS At this point we need to review the history of the relations between science, philosophy, and the law.

Briefly: we are living at the end of a cycle that began, to my knowledge, with Leibniz's *Theodicy,* although doubtless its roots go back to the beginning of history, to the foundation of the world. Let's ask its questions: What about pain, injustice, disease, famine, death—in short, those things we summarize under the name of "evil"? Better yet, and apparently more efficiently and justly, *can we designate who is responsible for these?*

In the preceding remarks, when we said, "It no longer depends on us that everything depends on us," can we cite the one or ones,

singular or collective subjects, designated by the recurring, familiar *us* or this strange *it?*

*BL This last way of posing the problem is what opened the era of criticism
we were talking about in our last session.*

MS Yes, an era of criticism, because it instituted a long succession
of tribunals before which were played out an equally long series
of trials. Indeed, this case dates from our origins, but its modern
formulation dates from Leibniz. The judicial action has remained
stable for three hundred years, the only change being in the
names and persons occupying the respective places of accused,
lawyer or defender, juror or plaintiff. In the *Theodicy,* the philosopher appoints himself the lawyer, by also taking the name
Paraclete, the Holy Spirit, and exonerates God of the accusation
of being responsible for evil—proof that the author also occupies
the place of judge. Since then this critical or even judicial orientation, far from failing, has grown, moving from legal action to
pretrial investigation and to the police inquiry that precedes it, or
toward the role of detective.

Today its naïveté seems even more naive than my own, which
you call a-critical. Because it is based on the postulate that one or
more subjective or collective beings responsible for evil, for suffering, for injustice, etc., surely exist—without asking any preliminary
questions about the very place of the accused.

*BL You're saying that we must continue to think about the problem of evil
but no longer in the way that criticism has done, seeking someone to accuse.*

MS Yes. Essentially, even if criticism does not believe in God, it
still believes in His place. It no longer believes that there is a God
who created the world, but it does believe that there are one or
more producers of evil—Satan or a hundred demons, replace-
ments, or substitutes. As a result, criticism puts in this place all the
usual accused parties, whose names we learn and pass on—males,
fathers, exploiters, whites, Westerners, logocentrism, the State, the
Church, reason, science—each one of which, surely, and often
heinously, is deeply implicated in this affair.

*BL Yes, denunciation—the processes of denunciation—seems impossible
to us. A lot of people have had this same intuition. By why should this
cycle finally culminate, according to you?*

MS Here's what's new: this cycle is ending for the obvious reason that it has exhausted the list of possible accused parties—the small change remaining from the former single accused party, the God whom the *Theodicy* put in the place of Satan, the former author of all evil. Each one of us, and finally everyone, will have his turn as accused: "...It's Voltaire's fault, it's Rousseau's fault..." Who is next in this carousel of finite substitutions?

You could even say that this list, which today is closed, is symmetrical to the list of former victims. The male was once the victim of the tempting female; today she takes his place, and so on. Inversely, some recent historical experiences of rapid replacement—of the male by a female, of an exploiter by a tyrant, of one thesis by its opposite, of a victor by his former victim—without there being any notable change in the ravages of evil, give the cycle an unexpected symmetry, as though the eternal return comes around again.

So, in the balance everyone can equally accuse himself, be accused, be exculpated, be exonerated—all equally justly.

BL If we have exhausted the possibilities for accusation, how would you define this new phase, which finishes (in both senses of the word) denunciation?

MS By this global result: evil, hate, or violence has every object but no subject. Rain, hail, and thunder fall on everyone, without there being a hand that dispenses them or controls the electrical current. Active evil is conjugated like an impersonal verb: it is raining, it is freezing, it is thundering.

BL But this it—*if it is no longer anybody, who is it?*

MS Everyone and no one. We are coming back to objectivity but, as I just said, from the other side of the universe, from the side of the social sciences.

So—everyone and no one. From a permanent and fluctuating cloud, injuries fall on all heads and on every head, indifferently. So, it remains to question the problem of evil in its entirety.

The Impossible Inquest

BL I don't see how the social sciences are responsible for this forgetting of the problem of evil, or for its perpetuation.

MS No doubt it is less the fault of the social sciences than of philosophical criticism, which relies exclusively on them and which sometimes assembled formidable mechanisms of accusation. These machines are ideologies. And in these they deceive themselves. Not in what they say, which is often right and justified, but in what they are. Admittedly, the exploiter exploits unjustly. Admittedly, certain people remain criminal because of thirst for power and glory, strength and victory. Admittedly, I have met a thousand times, as I'm sure you have, those who are bastards and abusers, parasites and killers. Admittedly, we have felt the heel of horrible pressure groups, crushing everything in their path, often in the name of seeking truth, justice, and morality, but they mega-deceive themselves (if I may say so) in their construction—in posing the question in terms of criticism, justice, trial, judicial action, and accused party.

BL This harks back to our last conversation, on the end of the critical parenthesis. Is it because of this that you no longer believe in criticism?

MS It's all tied together. We are all accused, accusers, denouncers, capable of being suspected and presumed guilty—but also presumed innocent. The problem of evil is no longer capable of being solved by judiciary action but becomes a scientific problem—universal, once again objective, stable, and recurrent in history—thus capable of being solved with neither individual nor collective subjectivity, but objectively. As impersonally as impersonal verbs.

So, morality is rational and universal, whereas perhaps ethics depend on cultures and places and are relative, like customs. Ethics are aligned with ideology, and morality is aligned with science: it's objective.

BL And the situation is changing today?

MS Reason made some progress between the era when crowds immolated a sacrificial victim and the critical era, in which a trial is held. Now it is taking another step forward.

Inquests are becoming exhausted because every possible defendant has sat in the accused's box, starting with Satan, one of the earliest to be charged, and then, symmetrically, God himself, right down to each of us, the rich after the miserable, the powerful after he who, exuding servile obedience, conditions the former before suffering at his hands—male and female, savage and civilized, ignorant and learned. All these trials have been reasonable, and the condemnations have been admittedly just, but, for all this, evil has not varied in the least and continues to spread its ravages.

BL So, all the accused have been redeemed?

MS And reciprocally. The cycle culminates; its balance sheet is perfect. What remains is Evil, in its sum—a cloud carried on the winds.

The fact that, essentially, we are all responsible gives a nice rational version of original sin. Do you know of any philosophy that doesn't contain, somewhere, an equivalent of this?

We could have predicted this passage from the judicial to the objective, since it goes from the case to the thing—*de la cause à la chose*—as though our very language knew it. We are all both the cause and the object of evil, which in turn is everyone's thing. Thus, it is universal and objective, simply there, thrown in front of us (who are thrown in front of it), exhibiting the characteristics of a scientific object. We learned this more quickly about bad weather, infectious diseases, pain, and death, for which we have not held anyone responsible for a long time (except for germ warfare). We even learned this about famine, for which it's a question of climate and of clouds carried by the winds. We have yet to learn it, painfully, about conflicts, injustice, and misery.

BL Are you saying that, in reaching the culmination of denunciatory legal actions, we are still not powerless? We are not reduced to quiescence? We are not impotent in the face of misfortune, injustice?

MS Perhaps not. Let's not move on so fast. Evil comes not so much from one Being or some beings, or from this or that particular one, as from relationships. As master of the world, Satan had or has relationships among people. The *morality* of relations is based on the *science* of relations.

Just as the virtual community of mankind takes the world as its common correlate of knowledge and of actions regulated in common (science), or as its partner in a natural legal contract, so this same evolving community henceforth can (and therefore must) take evil no longer as an inquest to be pursued but as a problem to be resolved.

BL But is this a question for science and the law and not for morality?

MS Certainly. Just as henceforth we should enter into a natural contract with the entire Earth, cannot we likewise enter into a new moral contract with the global collectivity of humanity, proscribing all accusation?

This contract and this proscription open the rational era in morality, in which we pass from the inquest to the problem.

I said a little while ago that the problem of evil was located at the foundation of our knowledge: this is the very point at which they touch.

The Foundation of Virtue

BL I understand this slippage. Before, we hoped to extricate ourselves from evil through the defeat or elimination of the accused party. Now we immerse ourselves in it for good, as we are immersed in the atmosphere or in time, since there is no more accused party to vanquish. But, at the same time, you take away our springboard to action. In objectifying evil, can we still act?

MS Let me answer with two examples. *In the collective:* without of course being able to demonstrate it, I have often had the intuition that in social or moral matters there is a sort of *constant* that cannot be evaluated, analogous to the one defined by the first principle of all mechanics and by thermodynamics. There is a terrible and secret equation between the unjust and abusive deaths and tortures produced by a tyrannical empire and the cadavers left by the tribal hatred and warfare in the same empire when it breaks apart, so that the same amount of violence seems to be conserved at the heart of any given human distribution. This experience is so frequent that it accompanies my entire life and illuminates my knowledge of history.

What we lack in order to demonstrate this is knowing how to calculate the appropriate distribution. It's as though evil re-

mained, changing its mask and its character, but always keeping
the same power and always producing, in total and on balance, the
same volume or the same sum of devastation.

Now, we know that a constant of this kind always founds its
corresponding science, because no one can think without somewhere depending on an invariable that underlies variations.

BL So, in this sense, there exists some "first principle" of evil?

MS I believe so. Thus, all morality and perhaps all of politics
consists first of recognizing such a principle head-on and of inventing, at best, ways of freezing and immobilizing this virtuality
that is continually on the lookout, always present and ready to
unleash the devouring hounds of its formidable effectiveness. Morality consists of watching over these freezing processes with the
same wise gaze as over the explosions. No political system is ex-
empt from this, either in its essence or its constitution.

*BL So, it is a question of managing and displacing constant quantities
of evil rather than remedying them? You're painting a bright future here,
I must say.*

MS Along the same lines I outlined in *The Parasite,* we must always
reformulate this question: What is an enemy, who is he to us, and
how must we deal with him? Another way to put it, for example,
is: What is cancer?—a growing collection of malignant cells that
we must at all costs expel, excise, reject? Or something like a
parasite, with which we must negotiate a contract of symbiosis? I
lean toward the second solution, as life itself does. I'm even willing
to bet that in the future the best treatment for cancer will switch
from eliminating it to a method that will profit from its dynamism.

Why? Because, objectively, we have to continue living with can-
cers, with germs, with evil and even violence. It's better to find a
symbiotic equilibrium, even fairly primitive, than to reopen a war
that is always lost because we and the enemy find renewed force
in the relationship. If we were to implacably clean up all the
germs, as Puritanism would have us do, they would soon become
resistant to our techniques of elimination and require new armaments. Instead, why not culture them in curdled milk, which sometimes results in delicious cheeses?

BL That's a fairly good solution to the debate on debate that has been ongoing in these conversations. Fond as you are of mixtures, you didn't like discussion—which still surprises me.

MS Let me say again that you have convinced me, in part, on the question of debate. The entire question of evil is to a certain extent projected into it. So, then, what is the enemy? Often a collection of partners that I have myself produced and with whom I am conditionally and continually obliged to contract.

The kind of debate that you are right in praising allows for a series of local contracts, represented here by segments of questions and answers. Whereas the kind of debate that frightens me produces a war that continually flares up more and more violently, going from local skirmishes to mortal advance-guard and rear-guard battles. Thanks for curing me of my formidable naïveté. (Is it possible that the monsters of our lives can sometimes be reduced to beautiful princesses, trapped inside frightening appearances, calling out to us for help?)

BL But, if we return to the individual level, I still don't see how to draw a rule for living from this objectification of evil.

MS In reading over the marvelous and detailed list of capital sins—those fundamental vices or neuroses that psychology explains so poorly (pride, greed, envy, gluttony, lust, anger, sloth)— who can help seeing that *growth* brings them together and makes them into functions, in the mathematical sense? The proud person wants only first places and, by living in the pure ordinal number, transforms the world into perpetual olympiads, with misfortune to the vanquished. The miser follows the cardinal series of numbers, from millions to billions, without being able to stop, with death to the wretched. Likewise, Don Juan runs up a list of over one thousand conquests—*Mille e tre*. The sloth prolongs his nap in order to clothe his life in a passive night, dominating his family and neighbors with his growing inertia. Neuroses are repetitive and always the first to be served, as are inclinations to vice.

Thus, virtue consists (and perhaps *only* consists) of stopping this growth. It's restraint exercised on oneself, reflexively, and the investing of a party with the power to restrain its power—a kind of *auto-restraint.*

You see how morality is distinct from exact reason while using its concepts very exactly.

BL So, you are not afraid to speak of virtues! But examples are not enough, in philosophy.

MS I'm talking about objective morality; everything that is objective is expressed in the third person. And the ensemble of everything expressed in the third person can be called—universal.

BL The third person? Having talked about prepositions in our third session, do you want to talk now about personal pronouns?

MS Yes. In order to make philosophy's telegraphic language of infinitives and substantives reliable, isn't it necessary to complete it?

In order to establish the objective morality whose two conditions I just described (the first coming from the hard sciences and technologies, the second from the other center, from the humanities)—in order to understand them together—I am seeking to formulate a philosophy of personal pronouns.

First, let's go back to accusation. It goes without saying that in the law we debate about cases or *causes* and in the sciences we debate about *things,* although it sometimes happens that the former are transformed into the latter, and vice versa. Our French language reflects this, designating them by almost the same word, gliding gently from one meaning to the other. From the Latin *causa,* the source of *accusation,* comes both the word *chose* (thing) and objective *causality.* We rediscover the third person.

So, to begin with, let's leave the recent and less recent reflexive and solipsistic philosophies to their quarrels over the subject of the cogito. Usually, in both camps it's a matter of transforming it into a noun, the *I, me, one, self.*

But, properly speaking, neither *I* nor *me* nor *you* in the singular (*thou*) is a pronoun—that is, a substitute for a noun. Rather, they are *tokens of presence* that the dialogue, dispute, debate, or account (direct or indirect) exchanges indefinitely. In support of this, may I refer you to pages 153–55 of my second Hermes book, *Hermès II. L'interférence,* written more than thirty years ago, and which I am correcting and completing now?

We need to consider the first-person plural in the face of the second-person plural, from which it separates itself in order to debate, and with which it is reunited through agreements—*we* and *you.* Now, both of these tokens of presence—exchanged between the groups during the course of the disagreement, the contract, or the war—cannot help but speak of the third person, without whom we would fall into silence or absence of thought. Therefore, let us redress the cogito, by relating the first-person (henceforth plural and easily englobing the second-person) to the third-person, which constitutes them both, thus:

WE SPEAK ONLY OF *HIM.*
WE THINK ONLY OF *HIM.*
FOR WE WOULD BE NOTHING WITHOUT *HIM.*

BL   I don't understand who this "him" is nor how he can be the objective foundation I asked you to give me.

MS The very one about whom we are speaking at this very moment. A third being, whom we expel from our linguistic sphere or seek to attract toward it—*him, the other, each one*—other people to whom we assign similar roles (*the others, everyone, them, one*), a collective either divided or taken together, partly or completely excluded from the circle of our linguistic family or, on the contrary, enhanced, glorified, or magnified through our suffix, *-ist* or *-ille*, the Latin pronoun from which we get the French *il,* "he"/"it." It is an object, plural objects—*that, this one, that one,* all or part of general objectivity. It is the impersonal world of physical meteorology: *it* is raining, *it* is thundering, *it* is hailing, *it* is snowing. Being-there, *Dasein* itself: *it* is, *there* is. And, finally, morality: *it is necessary to.* . . . Here we have an extremely complex and rich ensemble, whose sum should certainly be analyzed but whose diverse elements should also be integrated into one view.

It is thundering . . . it is necessary to . . . here no doubt we are dealing with the same *it* that begins the fundamental sentence: "It no longer depends on us that everything depends on us."

Taken in its totality, the third-person enunciates and describes at leisure all existing objectivity and all that is thinkable or possible—human, inert, worldly, worldwide, ontological, divine, and moral. This is what you were asking for—the foundation of objectivity in general, in sum and in its totality—the global referent for being and knowledge, for dialogue and debate, for the world and society, for what's subjective and what's impersonal, for love and hate, for faith and indifference, for things and causes—and not as a distant and passive spectator might speculate upon them, but in the dynamic and practice of collective or social action. You can see in this that *the foundation of morality is no different from that of physics,* which is what I wanted to show.

BL This singular him *seems somewhat plural to me!*

MS It's true. We never talk about anyone but him, whom we love or hate, as an individual or a group. We only ever think of him—the object of our desire, or love, or resentment. He is the fetish of our adoration, the stake in our conflicts, the commodity in our exchanges, the concrete or abstract support of our technical works or of our mediations. We never speak of anything but him, of the climate that bothers us or in which we are delightfully immersed, of the shelter that awaits us and into which we fear the storm may break. We never think of anything but him—absent and present in the universe, creator of the heavens and the Earth, of all that is visible and invisible. We never speak of anything but him, of the Being that inhabits us and does not let go of us. We never think of anything except him, of our duty, of the precept that for us makes the sun come up.

We will not survive without all of *them,* without this universe that is best designated by a third-person pronoun, since we do not know its real name, and since we are henceforth capable of constructing or destroying it at will—this compact, inert, living and human ensemble of produced *things* and conditional *causes.* Objective things (up front) and human causes of accusation or obligation (behind the scenes) are both produced at the same time.

BL Then I claim the same foundation for the social sciences.

MS Certainly. Chimpanzees and baboons (which you know more about than I since you have studied them), termites, or beavers—all animals continually enter into contracts among themselves that are purely social, empty, based exclusively on the concept of *us.* The simplicity of these pacts oblige animals to contract them in real time, continually. This is the well-defined, strictly political oppression in which animal societies are immersed. Humankind begins with the weight of the object, which is why the new social contract takes on a weight whose density opens up unexpected historical developments, rather than the repetition of the same contract.

Our contracts have *things* as their *causes*. Without things we would have remained political animals. But in the current state of affairs the so-called human or social sciences seem at best to apply only to animals.

Where *Things* Enter into Collective Society

BL I agree with you that the social sciences remain obsessed by subjects alone, by people interacting among themselves, and never speak of objects per se. But how do you introduce the object into these relationships? What myth can you propose?—for such a description must rely on myths, it seems to me.

MS Here it is. Neither *I* nor *thou* nor *we* nor *you* is a pronoun; rather, they are like wildcards in certain card games—multivalent and interchangeable jokers exchanged indifferently by certain relations. As a result, they remain precious notions for the collective itself and quite indispensable to the juridical disciplines, one of whose major functions is to define a subject of the law. The ego was first of all the subject of the verb *credo,* in the sense given it by Roman law and then by Christian theology, which is the source of its usage by Saint Augustine, from whom Descartes sprang. It remains a good legal and theological concept.

Probably the very first contract was empty and, being institutional, concerned only us. We were still animals, and we remain so still when, as political creatures, we remain caught in the dizziness of pure and simple relations. In such a situation, we only experience the eternal return of a law that has become formal or imaginary.

BL I'm still waiting for the appearance of the object.

MS So, then, along comes the first referent of the contract. For example, an apple—the one Eve gave to her first lover. A gift, a stake, a fetish, a first commodity, tracing heavily for the first time the relation of love, of disobedience, of knowledge, of risk, and of mad prophecy—this fruit brought about the first human collectivity, the simplest one in history. We discovered ourselves naked, lovers, mortal and sinful, standing already before the tree of science and standing already before a tribunal—divine, moral, civil, penal, deciding about good and evil—all because of this apple, *cause* and *thing*, the first object.

I neither can nor wish to cut up these multiple languages: philosophy speaks in several voices, as though in fugue and counterpoint; it uses a multivalent language, like mathematics; it expresses itself in polysemic parables and, through this pluralism, produces sense.

We would be nothing without *it/him/her*, and, from the beginning, we speak only of the third person. We don't talk about *any*thing, we don't think *any*thing if we don't think some*thing*, even if this some*thing* is the network of our relations—proof that *he/she/it* does not exist in the first-person if he/she/it does not exist *previously* in the third-person, even in our discourses.

The third-person is the basis of truth or meaning established verbally, in the sense that it gives them weight and stability long before giving them meaning and grace. No, discourse cannot be woven without it, since the third-person designates and describes the entire universe: men, things, God and being, climate and obligation—in sum, either the *causes* of the law and the *things* of science, or, definitively, the totality of our moral questions, both ancient and modern.

BL So the quasi object is a pronoun?

MS You are the one who brought it up!

So, this is how history went: it begins with the repetition of an empty contract, concerning only the fluctuating relations of the group. The first object makes the contract heavier and denser, and history, becoming more viscous, brakes and slows down, as though it were coming to a halt. Then the era of the law emerges, in which the only objects are stakes, fetishes, or commodities, marking the unanalyzable mingling of objects in our relations. Finally, science arrives, in which objects become detached from relations but construct new ones. This "feedback" between our relations and objects will never end.

BL So, the collectivity is produced by this double circulation of objects that create social relations and social relations that create objects. Nonetheless, morality does not come from this co-production of things and people?

MS The moral problems that weigh upon us today no doubt spring from our era when objects pilot relations, whereas we are just emerging from an archaic era in which relations piloted objects. Indeed, we must continually untangle the relations between the one and the other. We do not yet have an adequate idea of what the deluge of objects manufactured since the industrial revolution by science, technology, laboratories, and factories implies for our relations—and now for those universal relations brought about by our global enterprises.

We are certainly not mistaken when we believe in the objective usefulness of our products, but we never see clearly enough that they create tight interlacings of new relations, which are all quasi objects. Today, and perhaps ever since we became *homines fabri,* we have been working at fabricating some of these object relations. Henceforth we will produce the most global of these objects conditioning the totality of our relations, and which are the foundation of *obligation,* in the most obvious sense, *ties.* This is the reason for the globally objective state of morality; henceforth once we *make,* we *must.*

BL So, the conception of morality that you are developing here is linked to what we said earlier about the transcendental in relations—about this famous synthesis of the totality of relations, based on relations?

MS The totality of the causes of evil is the totality of relations. As we said before, to know what these are one has only to describe the network of prepositions.

BL For every quasi object there is a mode of relation, a preposition, and a deadly sin?

MS Yes. All of them, and each one expresses a portion of evil, and this is why God—whom tradition calls "the Good Lord"—is the sum of relations, with interest.

BL So, your philosophy introduces pronouns and prepositions into its language?

MS Why should philosophy continue to speak this telegraphic language consisting only of verbs and substantives, without any prepositions, without any declensions or pronouns, when without them we can express neither relations nor subjects nor objects?

In this new language, which is very close to everyday language, you will also see a whole new process of abstraction.

On Moral Law

BL To conclude your morality—we must distinguish it from ethics; we must modify the social sciences so they can absorb the objects of the hard sciences; parallelly, we must modify both the former and the latter so they can absorb the humanities, which carry the problem of evil, now objectified?

MS Yes, because we are entering the mixed zone of interferences we described earlier.

Meaning is born from evil and its problem, which crushes us. All by itself, violence sums it up. While ethics, which are close to the social sciences, take into account the multiple, diverse, and skewed options taken by cultures and individuals in their language and customs, universal morality (or "normal" morality, compared to the infinite number of skewed forms)—because it concerns the problem of objective evil, and because it is summed up in the question of violence—is in turn summed up in the commandment, "Thou shalt not kill," which we obviously retain, and in it alone: "Thou shalt not give thyself over to violence."

BL After having said in our preceding conversations that you seek synthesis rather than fragmentation, are you now going to go so far as to propose some laws?

MS Why should I shrink from it now?

The law used to be based on individual death; henceforth this law will be based on the eventual death of the human race and on the ensemble of specific global risks incurred. We have enough power to wipe everything out.

Thus, today the law becomes thrice universal:

  I. Thou shalt not give thyself over to any violence, not just against individuals, near or distant, but also against the global human race.
 II. Thou shalt not give thyself over to violence, not just against that which lives and lies in thy own backyard but against the entire planet Earth.

The commandment not to kill originally concerned people; from now on it also concerns the collective as such, and even, paradoxically, the inert, in its generality. In a new formulation, touching relations of defense, economics, and production, morality transcends the individual and the living in order to concern the collective and *things*, not simply in relation to a particular time, place, language, and culture, but specifically and integrally, because of the global power of our new military or industrial means, and because of the ensemble of paths henceforth discovered and exploited, from the local to the global.

III. Finally, thou shalt not give thyself over to any violence in mind, because, ever since the mind entered science, it has surpassed conscience or intention and has become the principal multiplier of violence.

This last law, which up until now has almost never been observed, concerns scientists, technicians, inventors and innovators, writers and philosophers—you and me.

BL So you still limit yourself to negative prescriptions?

MS No. Did you know that the French word *trêve* (truce)—which is what I am calling for—comes, even before old French, from a very ancient word meaning "contract"?

BL You are returning to the law.

MS More than that. Before organizing the good of others, which is often a matter of doing them violence, or harm, the *minimal* obligation is to carefully avoid doing them this harm.

The *maximal* obligation would consist, further, of loving not only thy neighbor but all global systems—individual, collective, living and inert. For this we need more than a morality—we need at least a religion. And on this question it's necessary to write—or read?—a new book.

Translator's Note

These conversations make repeated reference to Michel Serres's 1987 book *Statues,* in which he draws parallels between the explosion of the space shuttle *Challenger* at Cape Canaveral on January 28, 1986, and the ancient Carthaginians' practice of enclosing humans in a gigantic brass statue of the god Baal and incinerating them there, as a sacrifice to their deity (as described by Gustave Flaubert in his novel *Salammbô*). The similarities, according to Serres, include the immense cost to the respective societies in erecting these "statues," the active role of "specialists" (scientists/ priests) in setting the event in motion, the presence of a large crowd of onlookers, who witness the events open-mouthed in horror, and the repetitive nature of the event (replayed again and again on television screens; actively repeated in Carthage whenever national events seemed to require it). Other parallels Serres draws between the two events are the avowed goal (the heavens) and the fact that the statues, the brass deity and the high-tech rocket, were more than simple objects: they played a powerful social role.

Perhaps the most difficult for readers to accept is Serres's contention that denial played a large role in both events. Since the Carthaginians incinerated both animals and children in their statue of Baal, even the parents of the sacrificed children allegedly denied that the cries they heard were those of humans. "Those are not humans, but animals," they are quoted as protesting. We are engaging in a similar form of denial, according to Serres, when we say that the *Challenger* explosion was an accident; such accidents, he insists, are predictable, according to the laws of probability. Statistics detect in large numbers what we cannot perceive in individual cases. Thus, our technology contains shadowy areas of archaic violence.

The Baal/*Challenger* discussion recurs throughout the present series of interviews. For Bruno Latour's arguments against this comparison, see pp. 138–42.

Prep - 106
Nuclear Party - 132

'Percolator'
'Invention'
New laws (136)

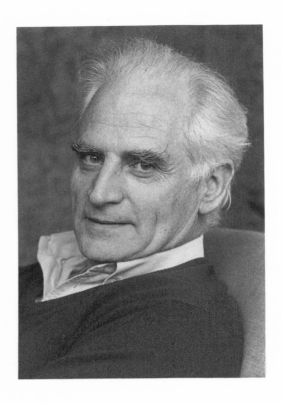

French philosopher of science **Michel Serres** has taught at Clermont-Ferrand, the University of Paris VIII (Vincennes), and the Sorbonne. He has served as visiting professor at Johns Hopkins University and has been a faculty member of Stanford University since 1984. His other works available in English translation include *The Natural Contract*; *Genesis*; *Rome: The Book of Foundations*; *Detachment*; *The Parasite*; and *Hermes: Literature, Science, Philosophy*. Forthcoming from the University of Michigan Press are translations of his works *Le Tiers-Instruit* and *Statues*. *Conversations on Science, Culture, and Time* was originally published in France as *Eclaircissements* and spent many weeks on the best-seller list. **Bruno Latour** is Professor of Sociology at L'Ecole Nationale Supérieur des Mines in Paris. He has written several books and numerous articles on the ties between the sciences and the rest of culture and society. **Roxanne Lapidus** is Managing Editor of *SubStance: A Review of Theory and Literary Criticism.*